THE ILL-FATED BATTALION

The Story of the 7th (Leith) Royal Scots at Quintinshill and Gallipoli

by

Peter Sain ley Berry

First published in 2013 by
ECW Press,
Llanquian House,
St Athan Road,
Cowbridge,
CF71 7EQ
Email: ecwpress@hotmail.co.uk

Printed by Antony Rowe Ltd, part of the CPI Group, Eastbourne

ISBN: 9781849144148

THE ILL-FATED BATTALION

This book is dedicated to all those soldiers who set out with such high hopes and who never returned.

Prologue

ROBERT KENNEDY,* the Caledonian railway signalman at Gretna Junction, was nearing the end of his shift. It was 6.20 am, the spring morning quiet and full of birdsong, the early sun burning off a distant haze.

He tapped the ashes from his pipe and from the high windows of his signal cabin looked out towards Gretna station. A jacket-less porter was shifting milk churns anticipating the imminent arrival of a local train that the railwaymen called the *'Parly.'* For Kennedy this train would bring the day's newspapers with their reports of the war.

The telephone rang, shrill in the quiet morning. It was George Meakin, his night signalman colleague at the Quintinshill signal box a mile and a half to the north, saying that he had decided to side-track the *'Parly'* at Quintinshill to let pass two late-running London expresses. This would also be convenient for his day colleague, James Tinsley, who lived at Gretna. 'The boy will get a ride today,' said Meakin.

* His real name was Robert Kirkpatrick but I have changed this to avoid confusion with the signal box to the north of Quintinshill which is also called Kirkpatrick.

5

But as he replaced the receiver Kennedy could see no sign of Tinsley. The bell rang in the signal cabin, three loud bells followed after a pause by a fourth. The *'Parly'* was approaching Gretna and the signal box to the south was asking him whether the line was clear. He signalled back that it was and entered the time in his train register book.

Not long after the signal bell rang again, this time one beat followed by two. The *'Parly'* had now entered that section of the line controlled by the southern box and so Kennedy rang through to the Quintinshill asking in turn for a *'line clear'* signal. When the acknowledgement came he pulled off his signals and again recorded the times in his register book.

The clock in the signal cabin was showing 6.25 when Kennedy caught sight of the *'Parly'* drawing round the bend on the approach to Gretna station. It was a small train, composed of two carriages plus milk and brake vans, yet it was hauled by one of the largest locomotives on the whole Caledonian railway. No. 907 of the Cardean Class usually pulled express trains, but she had just been overhauled and was now being 'run-in.' She had also been repainted and this morning looked immaculate in her livery of light ultramarine blue, lined out with black and white.

The train slid into Gretna station and Kennedy could see the porters loading churns of milk. A few passengers got on. Steam hissed from the big engine's safety valves. He saw the slight figure of Tinsley, who lived in a

6

railway cottage just across the line from the station, and opened the window of the signal cabin to gesture for him to get on the train. Clutching his sandwich box Tinsley ran across to the engine and climbed on the footplate. The train started and as it passed Kennedy's box he could see the fair-haired Tinsley leaning back against the tender.

He completed the signalling and entered the times in his book before turning to rake the dead coals from the fire. Now that the *'Parly'* had passed the two expresses would not be far behind. These left London's Euston station at 11.45 and 12.00 midnight and were due out of Carlisle at 5.50 and 6.05 am. Sometimes they ran late, held up by wartime traffic. They were running late today, which is why the *'Parly'* had been despatched ahead of them and why Meakin intended to side track the train to let them pass.

Kennedy signalled the first express, bound for Edinburgh, to Quintinshill at 6.33. It passed his box three minutes later in a cloud of steam as it tackled the rising gradient. He watched it disappear up the line and over the Border into Scotland. Eleven minutes later, at 6.47, he asked clearance for the second express, this one bound for Glasgow. This request also was granted.

At the same time Quintinshill asked clearance for a southbound troop train, which Kennedy accepted. This train appeared on his daily schedule of trains though he could see that it, too, was running late.

The second express passed, hauled by two engines. A long train of 13 carriages filled with many Scottish troops

7

returning home on leave. The train shook his cabin as it thundered past and headed for the Border.

Kennedy now waited for the troop train and looked northwards in expectation. One minute passed, then two, and then another two. Still there was no sign. Troop trains were given priority over other traffic so Kennedy wondered what might have become of it. Crossing to his signal bell he sent a single beat to Quintinshill, signifying a query. But no reply came.

Eventually the bell did ring. Kennedy counted six beats - the 'obstruction danger' signal - and immediately he raised all his signals. He then picked up the telephone to Quintinshill.

No-one answered. Two or three minutes went by. Then he recognised Tinsley's voice and heard himself asking, 'where's the troop train, Jimmy.'

Tinsley replied quite calmly, 'there's a smash up here.' Then he replaced the receiver.

Kennedy rang again. This time Tinsley's voice sounded hysterical. 'Send for the platelayers, send for the stationmaster, send for everybody,' he shouted.

ONE

Exactly a month before the fatal crash, on 22 April 1915, Provost Malcolm Smith had presided, as usual, over the regular Thursday meeting of the Leith Town Council.

The ten councillors and four bailies listened while Provost Smith told them that the town's territorial battalion, the 7th (Leith) Royal Scots, would be leaving the town next Saturday. He said Lieut. Colonel Peebles, their commanding officer, had told him the battalion was due for training prior to departing overseas on active service.

This departure should not pass unnoticed, the Provost said, and the councillors agreed. He proposed therefore that they should, on this Saturday, present each of the men in the four companies of the battalion with a cigarette lighter and a packet of cigarettes. One of the councillors quipped that the battalion should now me known as the 'Matchless Seventh' as none of them would have any further need for matches.

Today Leith is a suburb of Edinburgh but a hundred years ago it was a separate town, proud of its identity, that had grown up around its port, then the chief seaport of the

9

eastern lowlands. As trade expanded, a string of settlements grew up along the southern shore of the Firth of Forth, all the way to Musselburgh, and Prestonpans in the east and taking in the villages of Portobello, Joppa, Fisherrow and Inveresk. Seventy thousand men, women and children lived in these settlements and in Leith itself and it was from these communities that the territorial soldiers of the 7th (Leith) Royal Scots were recruited.

These thriving communities had grown up around the port and provided its labour. Many of these Royal Scots came therefore from the shipyards, where in 1915, more than two thousand men were employed, and also from those industries ancillary to shipbuilding and the docks: marine engineering, timber, wire rope and canvas manufacture, railways, leather, gas and a host of service trades. Leith's economy could even boast an early artificial fertiliser plant.

So when the town councillors and the bailies and the Provost of Leith turned out that Saturday morning to meet the battalion paraded on the platform of Leith Central station, they did so with pride and confidence. Leith was a success and this battalion would acquit itself with honour fighting for King and Country just as its predecessor had done in South Africa fifteen years before. The Royal Scots had always been the first foot regiment of the British Army and the current generation of soldiers would live up to this proud tradition.

The Provost made a short speech to which Colonel Peebles replied effusively. He was confident that the town would be proud of its men when they returned. Morale everywhere was high. The *Leith Burghs Pilot,* the local Leith newspaper, described the occasion as *'light-hearted, more like the departure of a picnic party than the setting out of a battalion for war.'* It was indeed to be some picnic.

****

Two hours later the 7th Royal Scots arrived at their training ground some forty miles away in Stenhousmuir, near Falkirk. Here they would be learning the advanced techniques of trench warfare and practising signalling and communications under fire. They would be training with the 4th Royal Scots, another territorial battalion who, soon enough, they would be fighting alongside. In the great tented city that became temporary home to these two battalions, the talk in the evenings centred on where they would be going. The widespread assumption favoured Flanders, but to which sector they had no idea. Ypres perhaps.

There was somewhere, else too. Sitting in their tents and perusing the newspapers they began to read about a place none of them had heard of before - Gallipoli - on Turkey's western edge. The allies had landed there just a few days before and the accounts in the newspapers of the brutality of the assaults and the heroism of the participants seemed beyond comprehension.

An old river steamer, the *River Clyde,* had been used to disembark soldiers under a murderous fire from Turkish machine guns. Great holes had been cut in the steamer's sides to make it easy for the troops to climb out and into lighters which formed a bridge to the shore. But so concentrated did the fire from the Turkish guns become that these great holes filled up and became choked with the dead and the dying. Piles of dead young soldiers had filled the bridge of lighters, the reports said.

All this had taken place under a bright and hot sun with the sea as calm as a mill pond. The ripples that did reach the shore were tinged with blood.

But the newspaper had not dwelt on the machine guns and the deaths, for it wanted to focus on the heroism of the 5th Battalion of the Royal Scots who had played a leading part in the landings. The men of the 7th Battalion wondered whether they would ever be as resolute under such fire.

Gradually the feeling grew among the soldiers that they would follow their colleagues out East. This grew to a certainty when the troops were issued with tropical pith helmets which some of the older members of the battalion remembered from the South African wars. Gallipoli it was then. But when?

They hadn't long to wait. Finally the announcement arrived that the two battalions, the 4th and the 7th Royal Scots, would depart from Larbert in four trains early in the morning of Thursday 20th May 1915. Then this was countermanded. There would be 48 hours of delay. Saturday 22nd May 1915, then.

TWO

The 4th battalion left first in the small hours of the night. The third train, due to leave at 3.45 am would carry 'A' and 'D' companies of the 7th Battalion. 'B' and 'C' companies would leave an hour and a half later.

Despite the early hour, Larbert station was crowded with well-wishers. Some were relatives, but many were ordinary people from Stenhousmuir and Falkirk who had been impressed by the soldiers they had been hosting for the past month and felt that their departure overseas should not pass unnoticed.

A group of friends had travelled up to Larbert from Bo'ness. east of Edinburgh, to wave off three companions who had all joined the battalion together in the heady days after the Declaration of War. Private Donald Porteous, an apprentice bookbinder from Edinburgh, who had celebrated his eighteenth birthday by transferring from the reserve battalion to 'A' Company, was one of these three along with Privates Andrew Williamson and Thomas Burnett

Another of those on the platform that morning was a miner from Niddrie, a village to the East of Edinburgh. Mr Hendry came with a present for his son who was in the battalion; two presents in fact; a shamrock charm and a lucky farthing. Private Hendry attached these to the identity disc that hung around his neck.

Similar charms and mementoes, souvenirs and keepsakes were passing between crowd and soldiers elsewhere on the platform as out of the dark night, the train that was to carry them to Liverpool came steaming into Larbert station. Slowly it came down the platform, the soldiers feeling the blast of heat from the furnace as the locomotive passed them and halted in a swirl of steam. The tang of oil and sulphur hung in the air. Behind the engine clattered the fifteen carriages for the soldiers and five trucks for their stores and behind this a six wheeled brake van

Red-eyed from lack of sleep the soldiers climbed aboard the fifteen carriages, throwing great coats and kitbags and rifles into the compartments. Eight men were allocated to each including an NCO in charge, but the accommodation was short and ten soldiers piled into some compartments.

Only four of these coaches had corridors. The remaining eleven were small six wheelers without bogies or lavatories or any way of getting from one third class compartment to another. The conditions were suffocating said one of them later.

In the rush Corporal Wood, a Leith man from 'D' company, struggled into a compartment in the middle of the train and found that only three of his platoon had followed him. Four others belonged to a neighbouring platoon commanded by another corporal, who now offered to exchange places with him. But Wood had settled

circular fastening on her smokebox cover, made of burnished steel, resembled a star.

On the footplate of the Dunalastair, Driver Frank Scott now set his controls for the ascent out of the Clyde valley towards the summit at Beattock. An experienced driver with 38 years service on the Caledonian, he had been selected to drive Royal trains on previous occasions andhad driven both Queen Victoria and King Edward VII.

Stoking the locomotive's ever hungry furnace was Fireman James Hannah, who had been with the Caledonian since leaving school at the age of 14. Though still a young man, he had been passed as a driver as and when there might be a vacancy.

Hannah had to shovel hard to maintain steam pressure in the boiler on the climb up to Beattock Summit, high on the southern Scottish moors and more than 1,000 feet above sea level. With a train of 300 tons behind, the Dunalastair laboured up the gradient.

The light was stronger now although it would be another hour before they would see the sun rise. Fifty miles of running would take them to their next stop - Carlisle.

Once over Beattock, the train descended the picturesque Annan valley with the meandering river a mile or two to the west. Past Dinwoodie and Hangingshaw they went, and past Auchenroddan forest to the east which marked the beginning of a four mile straight which would take them to the Dryfe water - an Annan tributary - and the run-in to Lockerbie.

Through Lockerbie they thundered, its folk then beginning to stir with the break of day; past the ruins of Malls castle and then across another Annan tributary, the curiously named *Water of Milk*. With a brief touch of the vacuum brake, Driver Scott slowed the train for the tight left hand bend around the hillock known as *Mainhill* and now, on an easterly course, they ran past Ecclefechan before swinging right again again on to a southerly course.

By now they were past the Annan and descending the valley of the *Kirtle Water,* and so over embankments and through cuttings to Kirkpatrick-Fleming. The speed of the train was increasing again as it entered the almost straight three mile stretch on a falling gradient of 1 in 200 which would take it on to Quintinshill and the last bend before the Border.

Scott had made up some lost time but he kept his speed down to sixty miles an hour, unwilling to take any chances with his old six wheeled coaches, and Hannah was able to take a rest from his stoking.

By now they were running almost due east and the newly risen sun was shining directly into the eyes of driver Scott. He tried to peer through the large triangular forward windows of the Dunalastair cab. He was looking out for the distant signal some thousand yards north of the Quintinshill signal box. Yes, there it was, showing clear. Beyond it he could now see the granite overbridge which he knew lay just a mile and a half north of the English border. And framed in the arch of the bridge he could just make out Quintinshill's home signals. he noted that they too were showing clear. Inside two minutes they would be over the Border and commencing the run into Carlisle.

FOUR

Robert Scott Finlay, a captain in the 9th Argyll and Sutherland Highlanders, had survived more than three months in the Flanders trenches. For the last thirty-four days he had found himself, almost continuously, in the battle line as his Dunbartonshire territorials had fought to contain the German advance around Hill 60 - an otherwise undistinguished mound on the Frezenburg ridge.

To his north a French army had been forced to retreat before a cloud of deadly chlorine gas and five British divisions, outnumbered by more than two to one, had been left with no alternative but to follow. Yet two miles outside Ypres they had dug in and counter-attacked. Finlay's battalion colonel had fallen and for a time Finlay had been left in command of the battalion, urging them forward until the thrust of the German advance had been reversed.

The counterattack had been successful but, with nearly 60,000 casualties, the five British divisions had been terribly mauled. Seven hundred of these were from the 9th Argylls who were now reduced to 315 men. This remnant were now relieved to be able to return to the reserve trenches. It was Thursday 20 May 1915. Some lucky fellows might even be allowed home for a few days rest.

The officers drew lots. One captain and two lieutenants might be spared, but only for four days, Captain Finlay and Lieuts. Kirksop and Bonnar were successful, packed and made all possible haste towards home.

They had reached London by three o'clock on Friday, there to celebrate in safety before catching the night sleeper home to Scotland.

At half-past eleven the officers made their way through the portals of Euston station and found their places in the front coach of the midnight sleeper - an elegant twelve wheeled sleeping car painted in crimson lake and cream and numbered 5132. Seizing the brightly polished door handles, they clambered in.

They were stowing their kit when Samuel Dwyer, the sleeping car attendant came to wish them a pleasant journey and asked whether they would like their early morning tea weak or strong.

Also in that sleeping car was a Mrs Nimmo, the young wife of a Newcastle draper. She cradled a baby in her arms. As they had only been able to obtain a single berth in that crowded train, Mr Nimmo travelled behind her in an ordinary compartment.

Lieut. Commander Head and Assistant Paymaster Paton shared a sleeping compartment, the latter travelling home to Glasgow on compassionate leave. His brother had recently been killed in Gallipoli.

Mr and Mrs Terryer took the next compartment and then came Herbert Henry Ford, the manager of William Arol's crane works at Parkhead, near Glasgow. Although originally from Bath, he had moved to Glasgow and now was returning to his home in Cambuslang after business in London.

The rearmost berth of the crimson sleeping car was taken by Mr and Mrs Macdonald, from Muswell Hill in London, who were travelling to Glasgow for a funeral.

In the following sleeping car travelled William Mackenzie, chief refrigerating engineer on the British India Steamship Navigation Company's ship, the *SS Carpentaria*. He had just a brought a cargo of refrigerated meat all the way from Australia, earning himself ten days leave, and was now returning with his wife to Greenock to spend it. Another merchant seaman, Captain James Williamson, general manager of the Caledonian Steam Packet Company, travelled behind.

There were some empty berths, too, for the Lord Provost of Glasgow, James Dunlop, who was in London with members of the Glasgow and West Scotland Armaments Committee, had booked six places on the train. But their discussions in the War Office had been lengthy and in the end they decided to stay in London another night. At the last minute they had cancelled their bookings.

They would have not stayed empty for long for crowds of troops and sailors home on leave thronged the station searching for a place on a train going north. The train guard - Philip Thomas - did his best to accommodate them, shuttling back and forth. Thus it happened that towards midnight Sapper George Robertson from Renfrew, resigned to not finding a seat on the train, made his way towards the front reasoning that it might be warmer there, being closer to the engine. Finding him there, Guard Thomas told him that he might find a seat in the last coach at the back, which, to his surprise, he did.

At the last minute a large party of sailors squeezed themselves on to the train. Ordered to remain in the rear coaches they nevertheless spilled out up the train. Thomas had to order them back repeatedly. Now sixty, Thomas had been a guard for 33 years, the last 14 of them spent on these West Coast expresses to Scotland.

But there were some he must have missed for Private James Richardson, a 19 year old gunner in the Royal Artillery, shared a compartment in one of the front coaches with others from his unit who were travelling home for a few days leave prior to embarking for France.

The soldiers and sailors standing in every available space irked those who just wanted to sleep. Three army motor transport drivers from Glasgow, who had actually found seats in the congested rear coaches, nevertheless found the train so crowded that one suggested they leave locomotives in Britain when first they made their appearance in 1903. Most express locomotives had four couple driving wheels, but the Cardeans had six, driven by two large steam cylinders and a boiler pressure of 200 pounds to the square inch. Engine and tender together weighed 130 tons. And in keeping with their special status, these engines carried a booming steam hooter instead of the usual whistle.

This engine, number 903, was being run-in after an overhaul prior to returning to express passenger work. In the workshops her Caledonian livery had been completely repainted and even her wheels were now painted blue with a white lining. The Caledonian crest, incorporating the arms of Scotland, stood out on the tender between the golden initials C R.

Usually the *Parly* waited to leave Carlisle until the two London expresses had passed. Only if they ran late would it be despatched before them and side-tracked later so they might pass. On Saturday 22 May 1915 the London expresses were running more than thirty minutes late and so the Parly was sent on its way ahead of them. The blue engine with its two scarlet and cream coaches, its milk van and brick red brake van puffed its way out of Carlisle's Citadel station and up the line towards Gretna.

Charles Forster, a young motor mechanic, was travelling in the third compartment of the second coach. He lived in Carlisle and was off to Lockerbie to pick up a vehicle. He had the compartment to himself. At Gretna station he looked out and saw the milk churns being loaded into the van and so did not notice the slight figure of James Tinsley coming round the side of the train and mounting the footplate beside the engine crew.

Soon they were off again. A whistle from Guard Graham, an answering blast on the Cardean's hooter, and the *Parly* train chugged forward on up the line and over the Border into Scotland.

and then they would come to the little river Sark that marked the actual Scottish border.

By this time the speed of the express was approaching sixty miles an hour and John Cowper swung himself across to the right hand side of the *Dunalastair* cab to ask David Todhunter over the clatter of the engine whether all was clear. The curving line made it difficult to see the Quintinshill distant signal from the driver's side of the cab. Todhunter confirmed that it was and threw another shovel of coal into the furnace while Cowper resumed his seat on the left.

Four sets of railway lines therefore ran in front of the Quininshill box, all being set on the low embankment and surrounded by pasture fields and hawthorn hedges dappled with pretty blossom, now just fading. Meakin though it made a pretty picture in the evening light.

That night Meakin was busy for the war had increased traffic on the railway by some 40 per cent and by the time the sky began to lighten Meakin was looking forward to the end of his shift. According to rule this should have been after ten hours, or at 6 am but he had come to an unofficial arrangement with James Tinsley, his relief, to change duty at 6.30. Such an arrangement allowed Tinsley to ride up to the Quintinshill box on the *Parly* train whenever this was despatched ahead of the London expresses.

But it was not an arrangement that would have been approved of by the inspectors (the box came under the supervision of the Gretna stationmaster and he had called three times in the last four days) and therefore, to keep it hidden, Meakin would sign the book as having left his duty at 6am and would write the signalling entries after that time on a telegraph form. When Tinsley arrived he would sign the register book as having come on duty at 6am and then copy these entries from the telegraph form into the train register book.

NINE

As the *Parly* arrived in front of the box Driver Wallace could see Meakin holding a green flag out of the cabin window - a signal that he should halt his train and then reverse it back through the crossover points. The train came to a slow halt two hundred yards further down the line with the brake van clear of the points. Wallace threw over the reversing lever and the little train began to snake through the points on to the up running line.

During this procedure, Thomas Ingram the guard from the goods train, entered the cabin. He was a man of middle age and thirty years of service on the railway. Meakin was at the lever frame, replacing the crossover points before going to the block to send the 'train out of section' signal to Gretna now that the *Parly* was no longer on the down line.

The two men greeted each other but Meakin had not much time time to talk. Looking north he could see that the train of coal empties had now arrived at the

51

Quintinshill up home signal some two hundred yards away. Meakin set the points for the up loop and then pulled off his up main to up loop signal. Puffs of steam from the locomotive, seen a moment before they were heard, announced that engine number 60 with Driver Benson at the controls was moving forward again, drawing the long train of empty coal wagons off the up main line and into the loop.

The *Parly* had by now come to a halt - just south of the signal box on the up line. James Tinsley thanked Driver Wallace and jumped down on to the ballast to make his way up to the cabin where Meakin - the train of coal empties by now safely in the loop - was just about to replace the up loop points and signal.

Meakin threw the levers over, all the while briefing his mate on the situation with the trains: that the expresses were running late and on what the foreman at the Kingsmoor yard had said about the lack of accommodation for the coal empties train there. Tinsley looked at the telegraph form to see what entries there had been since 6 am. He counted fifteen.

As they were talking the telephone rang again and as Tinsley had started to copy the entries on the telegraph form into the train register book so that they would show in his own hand writing, Meakin answered it. The call was from Kirtlebridge to say that the third of the four southbound troop trains had passed Lockerbie at 6.32, running some twenty minutes late. It would be passing Quintinshill in another fifteen or twenty minutes. No need for any immediate action. Tinsley could complete writing up the entries.

It was now about 6.35, though Tinsley had already written in the fiction that he had been in the box since 6 am. Meakin wiped his hands on some cotton waste and went to sit for a few minutes beside Thomas Ingram at the back of the box. He would leave in a couple of minutes and be home perhaps by 7am.

Now it was the turn of George Hutchinson, the fireman of the Cardean locomotive at the head of the *Parly,* to climb down from his cab and make his way across the tracks. The coal empties train had come to a halt and so he was able to duck down between two wagons to cross the loop line and so make his way to the signal box.

This was a visit prescribed by the railway regulations which said it was the fireman's duty to ensure that when his train was moved on to the opposite running line it was protected and that another train would not therefore run in to it.

Specifically the fireman was required to tell the signalman of the whereabouts of his train and then to ensure that the signalman had remembered to place a small iron collar over the signal lever controlling the appropriate signals. Such a collar was designed physically to prevent the safety catch on the signal lever being released and therefore to prevent the signal being activated. It was a simple device designed to ensure a busy signalman did not forget about a train placed in a loop or, in this case, on an opposite running line. The action was particularly relevant where the fireman's train might be out of the signalman's sight.

But for a relatively young fireman, such as George Hutchinson, to suggest to an experienced signalman, such a James Tinsley that he might forget about a train on whose footplate he had himself been riding only a few minutes before and which was standing in full view virtually in front of the signal box, might have seemed unnecessary. Besides, although lever collars were prescribed in the regulations, they were rarely employed, other than in situations where there were special circumstances in which a train - or more likely a wagon - might be forgotten in a siding or a loop.

The collars were in any case a back-up procedure: when a train was shunted on to the opposite running line, the signalman would send a signal on the block instrument known as 'blocking back.' In effect this told the signalbox in the rear that there was a train 'in section.' His block instrument would register this fact and this would prevent him from offering any trains forward.

So that morning Hutchinson did not see that collars had been placed over the safety catches on the up home and distant signals. He just signed his name in the train register book as the regulations required and assumed that Tinsley knew about his train. Which indeed Tinsley did, for he told Hutchinson that he would send the *Parly* on its way again as soon as the second of the London expresses had passed. Hutchinson then joined Meakin and Thomas Ingram on the bench at the back of the signal box.

Tinsley had arrived with that morning's *Daily Mail* and the railwaymen flipped through its news: an account of the destruction of Ypres, a reported offensive in Serbia, a report that Italy was now preparing for war. The leading article that Saturday continued the campaign for more shells to be supplied to the British Armies in France. The back of the paper carried pictures showing a German mine being exploded at sea and another of a dugout - named *'Le Moulin Rouge,'* full of French soldiers in festive spirit.

The signal box began to shake with the vibration of a fast approaching train. The railwaymen watched as the first of the two London expresses, this one Edinburgh bound, thundered past the cabin. It was 6.37 and the second, Glasgow bound express had just left Carlisle.

Now Brakesman William Young from the coal empties train came into the cabin to join the other railwaymen at the back of the cabin. He wanted to know how long they were likely to be kept. He was nearing the end of his shift, he said, and he wanted Tinsley to phone for a relief.

Hutchinson, his duty done, left the box to make his way back to his engine. Thomas Ingram accompanied him. But George Meakin remained in the box reading Tinsley's newspaper. A moment or two later, the bell rang on the block instrument controlling the up line. Tinsley was being offered the south bound troop train. He looked at the block - saw that it was clear - and acknowledged the bell, giving the line clear signal. Then, in a movement that he had performed so many times before, he pulled off his up line signals.

Three minutes later - at 6.46, he received the 'train entering section' signal from Kirkpatrick in respect of the troop train which he acknowledged and offered forward to Gretna.

The bells rang again - this time on the down line - in respect of the Glasgow bound express. Tinsley accepted this too, offering it forward to Thomas Sawyers at Kirkpatrick who accepted it in his turn. Tinsley now pulled off his signals for the express.

At the back of the box neither Meakin nor William Young paid any attention to his actions. The stage was now set for disaster.

TEN

In his compartment in the second coach of the *Parly,* Charles Forster, the car mechanic, began to fret. They had been stopped for a quarter of an hour now and he was growing impatient at the delay. One express had already passed on the up line and he wondered what they might now be waiting for.

Throwing aside the newspaper that he had brought with him from Carlisle, Forster lowered the carriage window by its leather strap, The sun shone brightly on that side of the train and he had to squint as he looked backwards in the direction they had come. Others were doing the same thing: he noticed the guard looking along the line and he saw a young woman looking our of her carriage window admiring the morning scenery beyond the wagons of the goods train.

Forster could see the bulk of the signal cabin on the far side of the train of empty coal wagons and noted with satisfaction that a figure clad in blue overalls was now emerging at the foot of the cabin steps. Forster saw the figure duck underneath the coal wagons and make his way across to the engine at the head of the train and climb on to the footplate. He even heard the man's boots crunching on the ballast between the tracks. Perhaps at last they would be moving off.

But the train didn't move. Tinsley intended to keep them there until the second express had passed. The fireman opened the fire hole doors and threw a couple of shovelfuls of coal on the furnace bed.

He looked up and through the large cab window along the blue painted boiler whose heat was making the air shimmer above it. From his side of the cab he could see clearly the two hundred yards to the Quintinshill home signals for the up line. He noted with horror that they were showing 'clear.'

Hutchinson, couldn't quite believe his eyes and called Driver Wallace over to check. If he thought then about the lever collars it was too late.

Charles Forster, still frustrated by the delay, looked out again, this time up the line to the north, the curve of the line giving him a clear view of the blue Cardean locomotive at the head of his train. If he noticed the Quintinshill home signals then he didn't know what they meant or to which lines they referred, but beyond the signals he could see a granite overbridge about four hundred yards up the line.

He was just about to return to his seat when he thought he noticed something silhouetted between the piers of the bridge. It seemed to be a train - Forster could see the sun's reflection on the burnished steel of a locomotive smokebox. At that distance of some five hundred yards its pace seemed leisurely and Forster assumed it would pass on the clear down line. Seconds later he thought he must be witnessing an optical illusion: the train appeared to be on the same track as his own.

On the Cardean locomotive, Wallace and Hutchinson saw the troop train approaching at the same time as Forster. They realised they would have no time to reach the signal box, but might just have a few seconds to scramble down from the footplate and to safety beneath the empty coal wagons.

Charles Forster also thought quickly. Finding the carriage door locked on that side of the train, he grabbed hold of the luggage racks hauling himself up and precipitating himself through the open window. He, too, rolled for safety underneath the closest coal wagon. Then came the crash.

The sound of the collision, people said later, was like a great gun firing. The air split in a reverberating crash. Like a maroon the sound signified disaster.

Three hundred tons of troop train that shortly before had been travelling at sixty miles an hour met the two two hundred ton *Parly* standing immobile with its brakes hard on. The two locomotives met, buffer to buffer, rearing up like horses and crashing across the line of coal wagons.

Having finished his paper George Meakin had actually left the signal box and was descending the steps as the troop train rushed by a few yards from disaster.

Horrorstruck, he watched the impact, the engines rearing up, the coaches of the troop train collapsing like concertinas. He rushed back up the stairs and into the box.

"Whatever have you done, Jimmy?" he shouted at Tinsley. But the latter, dumbfounded by the crash outside the box, couldn't speak; disbelief at what had occurred evident in his blank expression. His petrified eyes shot hunted glances at the signal frame and at the block instruments.

"The frame's all right .... and the signals are all right," he stammered, eventually. Meakin cut him short.

"You've got the *Parly* standing there!"

Tinsley continued staring alternately at the block instrument - that failsafe device design to ensure that this sort of smash could never happen and at the wreckage outside the box. Numbed by the enormity of what had happened the seconds ticked away.

Meakin's mind was numbed too. He, too, stared alternately at the up line block and then at the wreckage outside. He saw that the Cardean locomotive had slewed around, its great eight-wheeled tender now lying across the up main line. Suddenly, he remembered something.

"Where's the 6.5?" he shouted.

Without waiting for a reply, Meakin sprang to the signal frame and praying he was in time threw over the up distant signal, one thousand yards south of the signal box. Then he threw over the down home signals and rushed out of the cabin.

The up home signals - the fatal signals that had allowed the troop train to plough into the *Parly* - were still lying clear half an hour after the accident.

ELEVEN

The sound of the collision between the onrushing troop train and the stationary locomotive of the *Parly* could be heard for miles around.

In the Blacksmith's shop in Gretna Green, where eloping couples tied their hasty and often ill-considered knots, Mrs Dunbar, the caretaker, was already busy preparing for a Whit-Saturday rush of visitors from Carlisle. An endless series of weddings, the most recent only yesterday, kept her busy all through the spring and summer. She came out of the shop and on to the street and others did likewise asking themselves what could have caused such an explosion. Mrs Dunbar could only think that the Germans must have invaded Scotland.

But those nearer the line could see all too well what had happened. Andrew Sword laboured on Aitcheson's Bank Farm and had been out in the fields a good twenty minutes when, looking up, he witnessed the collision from two hundred yards away. He saw 3,000 gallons of water from the Cardean's great eight-wheeled tender, ruptured by the collision, pouring down the side of the embankment and into the ditch below. Sword remembered quite clearly the sunlight glinting on the cascade of water. It was still not seven o'clock.

Above the wreck of the engines he also saw great clouds of steam roaring out of the wrecks of both locomotives where the impact had sprung their boilerplates and cylinders.

Behind the locomotives the carriages of the troop train had simply concertina-ed, the ancient coaches just collapsing in the wreck, smashing themselves to matchwood. Those that didn't simply telescope seemed to take to the air and flew over the wreckage like steeplechasers, overshooting the locomotives and coming eventually to rest on their sides about the tracks beyond the locomotives. One coach lay on the empty coal wagons, another jumped these two and came to rest at the foot of the embankment. Moments before the fifteen carriages of the troop train had occupied two hundred yards of track; what remained took up less than seventy.

For a moment everything appeared quiet and still; even the initial hiss of escaping steam seemed to subside. And then, very slowly, little knots of soldiers began clambering out of the shattered train, dazed and distracted and most without boots. Andrew Sword could see their shapes between the wagons of the goods train. All over the up main line.

Away to his right he heard the rumble of a heavy train approaching at sixty miles an hour and there, maybe half a mile from where he stood, dazzling in the sunshine came two engines of fairy-tale blue, trailing long plumes of white steam and a train of scarlet and cream carriages. Racing up the line towards the wreckage which they could not yet see.

George Meakin had thrown the Quintinshill up distant signal to danger, but the seconds that had elapsed between the first collision and his remembering the Glasgow express, meant that it had already passed the signal post, a thousand yards from the cabin, by the time he had thrown the signal to danger.

Others with sharp wits also remembered the express. In his brakevan Guard Douglas Graham had been writing up his journal when the troop train had run into the *Parly.* He had been thrown violently forward, his head crashing against the wall of the van. Momentarily, he had lost consciousness; blood pouring from a head wound.

On the engine of the train of coal empties, Fireman Grierson and Driver Benson, heard the collision and watched in horror as the coaches of the troop train came flying over the engines and landed on their empty wagons. More than half a minute elapsed before one of them recalled that the Glasgow express was due.

From where they were they could not see the down distant signal which lay hidden in the cutting, nor did they have any way of knowing whether or not it might be at danger, or even whether the express had passed it. But they could both see the red home signal easily enough, and that showed a clear line.

So they clambered down from the footplate and began racing up the line as fast as they could run. Recovering from his fall Guard Graham also saw the clear home signal in front of him and behind him the dazed soldiers pulling each other free from the wreck and over the down line. He jumped down from the brake van and joined Benson and Grierson in a furious dash up the line. Three railwaymen were now running as fast as they could to warn the express.

Panting his way along the track, Graham realised that he had forgotten to pick up his red flag and his detonators. Placed on the railway line these would explode under a locomotive's wheels giving auditory warning of danger. Bruised by his fall and running with a heavy overcoat, Graham, who was far from being a young man, nevertheless made steady progress up the line. Over his shoulder he saw Benson and Grierson on the other side of the tracks, running hard as he was.

Less than half a mile away, Graham now saw the double plume of steam emerging from the cutting, the engines of the express swinging into the gentle curve that would take them up to Quintinshill. He was dismayed at the speed at which the express seemed to come on. When it was still a couple of hundred yards away, Graham halted, he had been running for nearly a minute, his heart pounded and his breath came in great gasps. He tore off his guard's hat, remembering that it had a red lining and held it outstretched in front of him, waving it and yelling. But speed of the heavy blue engines seemed undiminished.

They passed but as they passed came the roar of compressed air escaping from the Westinghouse air brake on the leading locomotive and the squeal as the brakes began to bind. Seconds later he heard a similar roar from as the train engine also locked its brakes.

"Please God I am in time," said Guard Graham to himself'

TWELVE

On the leading engine of the express Fireman David Todhunter had been shovelling hard to maintain pressure in the boiler as the engines pounded their five hundred ton train up the gradient at sixty miles an hour. By chance he glanced out and caught sight of Graham's cap. He could see men on the line too. he yelled to his driver.

"For heaven's sake, Jack, hold hard, there's something wrong." John Cowper had reacted immediately, slamming on the Westinghouse air brakes and throwing over the reversing lever to reverse the flow of steam to the cylinders. On the train engine Driver Andrew Johnstone had seen Guard Graham and was doing the same thing. Later he was to say that he thought they could have pulled up nicely in another 110 yards.

But they didn't have another 110 yards. Though their speed was falling rapidly, from 60 miles an hour to maybe 30, the first of the three coaches from the troop train that had overshot their engine was now only feet away. On the leading engine John Cowper could see soldiers on the line, focused on trying to rescue their injured colleagues from the wreck of the troop train, and completely oblivious to the inexorable progress of the express. Not bearing to face the sight he turned away his back to the front wall of the cab and braced himself for the inevitable.

The engines of the express hit this coach and the two wrecked coaches behind it, cutting through them as though they were paper. Tinsley was later to report that the he could hear the sound of the coaches being torn apart even in the signal cabin. Then came a more substantial blow and the front of Cowper's engine reared up while an avalanche of coal shot forward from the tender on to the footplate. Still moving forward, impelled by the 500 ton train behind it the engine fell back into the tangle of wreckage and, now derailed, slithered roughly to a halt along the ballast. Behind the engines the leading coaches of the express collapsed and telescoped.

Cowper was to learn later that the solid object that had caused his engine to rear like a frightened horse had been the sixty ton tender of the *Cardean* locomotive that had once pulled the *Parly* and which had slewed across the up line following the collision with the troop train. This tender had been carried down the line by the final momentum of the express, ripping open several upright and relatively undamaged carriages at the rear of the troop train - 'like a gigantic can opener,' said someone afterwards - and collapsing them towards the wrecked and telescoped carriages of the express.

Apart from the four engines, the wreckage now comprised a tight and compressed pile of largely featureless matchwood one hundred yards in length.

David Wallace, who with Fireman Hutchinson had leapt from the *Cardean* locomotive at the head of the *Parly* seconds before the troops train ran into them, was sheltering under the train of empty coal wagons. He saw soldiers emerging from the smashed train, some with grave injuries being helped by their colleagues. They were all about the train on both sides.

Wallace had experienced the same delayed realisation as the three railwaymen who had run up the line to warn the express, and he knew he had to warn the soldiers to stay clear of the up line. He could hear now the express coming on and he shouted and waved but the dazed soldiers, who had been asleep just seconds before and who were now trying desperately to rescue their colleagues, paid him no heed.

Many just looked uncomprehending as the express bore down upon them. Wallace remembered one young man. who had just hauled an injured colleague from the wrecked troop train, standing defiantly in the path of the oncoming express, refusing to let go of his injured friend and save himself, so that they were both cut down and both perished.

But even the blackest cloud can have a silver lining. A moment before the collision James Trainer, the seventeen year old drummer boy whose father carried messages at the Clydesdale Bank, had been asleep in one of the leading carriages of the troop train. He was to tell afterwards how there had been this terrible crash and how he had been thrown to the floor as the carriage had telescoped around him. Through the collapsing woodwork had come the butt-end of a rifle and this had pinned him down immobile. Several friends he saw also hopelessly trapped by the tangle of woodwork.

Now steaming water from the sprung plates of the troop train engine boiler started to trickle through the wreck and James Trainer said that he had cried out in pain as the scalding water had seared his side.

But then the second impact had come as the express had ploughed through the troop train wreckage. Everything shifted and suddenly James Trainer, the seventeen year old drummer, found himself free and able to crawl to safety.

But John Cowper, the driver from the leading engine on the express could not see this. He had braced himself for the collision by turning away from the tragedy and now found himself buried up to his neck by an avalanche of coal that had shot forward off the tender. The coal pinned him to the hot wall of the firebox and by the time he was rescued his back had been badly burned. David Todhunter, his fireman was luckier. He too had been caught by the avalanche of coal but it came only to his waist and he managed to free himself after a few minutes.

And it was not only coal in which they were buried for the engine itself was practically buried in broken wood and glass. Directly above them, precariously balanced across the roof of the cab, lay part of a carriage that had once belonged to the troop train. And in the angle between the wreck of this coach and the cab itself Cowper could just see the fatal home signals on the down line two hundred yards away: they were still lying off.

THIRTEEN

The two engines of the express both suffered serious damage in the collision: their frames had been bent and their bogies displaced and damaged. Behind them the front four coaches of the express had telescoped, the first sleeping saloon, No 5132 faring particularly badly. The remains of these coaches had become tangled with the wreckage of the troop train in a densely packed mass of wood, iron and glass in which many of the surviving members of the Royal Scots, and some of the passengers of the express, were now entombed.

Piled higher than the locomotives themselves, the wreckage lay compressed between the wagons of the two freight trains in the up and down loops, its centre some seventy yards south of the Quintinshill signal box and extending for about fifty yards on either side of this point. At the centre of this combustible mix, beneath the splintered wood and fabric, lay twenty tons of prime steam coal spilt from the locomotive tenders. And beneath this coal, where the firebars of the troop train engine had been shattered in the collision, burning coals now spilled on to the track from the locomotive's furnace. It did not take long for the fire to spread.

Elsewhere in the shattered wreckage flames of gas still burned, though no longer safely on incandescent mantles. Many of the gaslights in the twelve gaslit carriages of the troop train had been turned off in the morning light, but there remained plenty still burning, and these now caused further outbreaks of fire along the train.

Still pinned against the hot firebox by the avalanche of coal John Cowper noticed that the roof of the carriage lying on top of his cab was on fire. He could see the smoke rising in black smudges against the blue sky.

The shock of the second collision, when the tender of the *Cardean* locomotive had been dragged along the side of the troop train wreckage, sheared the coupling between the last coach and the six trucks that carried the battalion's ammunition and stores. Such was the force of this that the six trucks and the brake van at the end of the train were sent rolling backwards up the line.

William Young, the brakesman of the coal empties train who had followed George Meakin out of the signal box just before the first collision, thought immediately of his fellow brakesman and troop train guard, Charles Leggatt, and went to assist him.

By the time he caught up with them the trucks were rolling only slowly and he was able to leap on to the step of the brake van. Inside he saw Charles Leggatt, lying senseless on the floor, blood flowing from a head wound.

Taking a handkerchief Young staunched the flow of flood and was relieved when Leggatt opened his eyes, confused by the backward motion of the van. Young moved to the windlass and after a couple of turns the brakes bit and the collection of vehicles came to a gentle halt. There was little else left of the troop train that had left Larbert earlier than morning.

Young helped the older man out of the van and they began to walk back towards the signal box when a shoot of flame, six feet high, burst from the wreckage in front of them. Leggat said "look at that now, and there's no water."

A soldier ran up, hatless and without a tunic. Private Rennie remained the only uninjured member of the battalion's ammunition section. He had seen the first flames and thought of the ammunition trucks and the explosives they also carried. It would be important to secure them against rolling back into the fire.

With Rennie assisting, Young secured the brakes on each of the trucks and scotched the wheels with stones. As they were doing this other soldiers came up to break out the battalion's trench equipment and they forced open the trucks laden with picks and shovels, axes and cutting gear.

Young noted that several were without boots, presumably taken off for the night journey and now left behind in the wreck. These soldiers were treading painfully on the sharp ballast stones in their stocking feet and he saw that several had tied pieces of wood to their feet, the better to go about.

From the remains of the first class compartments in the rearmost coach of the troop train, Colonel Peebles emerged uninjured with several other officers to take charge of the situation.

Immediately he saw that many of the young soldiers, who had escaped injury, had been quite bewildered by the shock and the enormity of the situation and were now wandering around to no purpose, incapable of coherent action. Then he seized a pick and calling on a couple of soldiers to assist began to hack at the wrecked coaches.

From his position two hundred yards away in the field beside the line, Andrew Sword saw the express run into the the wreck of the troop train and heard the awful sound of the coaches telescoping and being thrown all around. He began to run towards the wreck, racing toward the railway line as though his own life depended on it. As he did so he noticed John and Andrew Mackie, the sons of his employer, who had been at breakfast in the Aitcheson's Bank farmhouse when the thunderclap of the collision had sent them rushing to the window. Now they were running hard across the fields as well.

The three men arrived practically together and noticed at once the flames beginning to lick out of the wreckage. The scene, as they described it afterwards, was one of complete devastation. All along the line of smashed woodwork arms and legs, heads and bodies, protruded grotesquely, some of them living, others dead. And hidden from view, from deep inside the wreckage, where some two hundred people lay trapped, injured and entombed, in the path of the fire, came heart-rending cries for assistance they could do nothing about.

Fire had indeed been the ogre at many past railway tragedies. At Quintinshill, few could have predicted its ferocity or the speed at which it spread. Fuelled by coal, by the gas carried for the train lighting and by the battalion's ammunition, the wreckage burned for a night and a day, and when finally it was brought under control, it wasn't as a result of the firefighters' efforts, but simply because there was nothing else left to burn.

FOURTEEN

Private Graham, the twenty year old soldier from Leith, awoke that morning to find the compartment he shared with seven other soldiers collapsing about him. The bench seats banged together trapping arms and legs, while the walls of the compartment caved in, the glass windows shattering. Graham found himself showered with glass and sustained a cut to his head. Everyone was pitched on the floor and their equipment came tumbling down from the luggage racks on top of them.

At first he was too dazed to do other than realise that he wasn't badly injured and for a brief minute he drew breath as he tried to ascertain what had happened.

He began struggling to free himself when suddenly the second collision raised the carriage on its end where it hung for a moment before crashing down again. For the second time Graham tried to wriggle free, but the coach started to move again and though he couldn't see what was happening he felt the movement as the wrecked coach slithered down the embankment before finally coming to a rest at the bottom.

He was now caught by the collapsing woodwork in an even tighter grip which threatening to crush his chest and Graham feared his ribs would burst. All around he could hear the cries and groans of injured soldiers, but he focused his mind on freeing himself. Looking around Graham could see grass beyond the shattered wall of the compartment and he found that he could stretch his arms just sufficiently to reach it. His fingers dug into the earth and he inched his body forward.

But only so far, for his legs remained fast - trapped by a heavy baulk of timber that he had no strength left to move. And so he lay, half in, half out of the smashed carriage, his head and shoulders in the bright sunlight and his body and legs in the tangle of the wreck.

Graham thus didn't see the Mackie brothers come up but he felt the pull of their arms. Now Andrew Sword took hold of a stout piece of timber and using this as a lever lifted the up some of the crushing woodwork. Slowly the two men pulled Graham clear of the wreck and carried him into the lineside field where he lay on his back, dazed and exhausted. Private Graham, thus had the distinction of being the first to be rescued from the troop train at Quintinshill that morning.

Sword and the Mackie brothers hurried back to the coach again, noticing more smoke at the top of the embankment above them and wondering whether this coach, too, would also soon catch fire; and so they hurried to find the next soldier and to drag him clear. The Mackies groped in the wreckage and were able to pull to safety a young Lance Corporal who had been in charge of Graham's compartment.

They laid him out beside Graham on the grass and as he observed the devastation above and around him he reflected that he would a thousand times rather have faced the Germans. "At least with them you have a bit of a chance," he said.

Finding no more men to rescue from this coach Sword and the Mackies were making their way towards the rear of the telescoped carriages, when a particularly sharp cry made Sword look up. Behind a shattered window loomed a face with blood dripping from a savage gash down the cheek from eye to jaw. "For Heaven's sake get me out of here." cried the man. Sword saw he was an officer and with the help of the Mackies they were able to get him out of the train.

The flames were taking hold of this coach, too, Sword could smell the choking reek of burning horsehair and see the occasional flame. He and the Mackie brothers worked fast and through the same shattered window they rescued two other officers. Battered, bruised and dazed by the collision they nevertheless did not seem too badly injured for Sword saw them later directing rescue operations among the uninjured soldiers.

Whether a fourth man they saw had originally been in the same compartment they had no way of telling for the interior partitions had collapsed entirely. This man was obviously injured and was groaning in pain. Sword laid a hand on him, but he yelled in agony and so Sword released him. The man's back was broken and he begged Sword not to touch him again.

But by now the fire was approaching fast and Sword realised that unless the man were moved he would be burnt alive. With the Mackie brothers helping thy smashed their way into the wreckage and ignoring the man's screams, carried him out and laid him out in the field beside the line.

When they looked back they could see that the flames had closed around the coach they had just left and Sword realised the sad plight of the many trapped and injured soldiers who must still be inside. Some of the young men called, not unnaturally, for their mothers. Andrew Sword reported one soldier lying crushed by the wreckage crying out to him: 'Oh tell my mother. Oh where is my mother?' But as Sword tried to assist him the soldier expired.

FIFTEEN

When David Wallace, the driver of the *Parly,* saw that fire had broken out next to the broken furnace of the troop train engine, he ran to collect four fire extinguishers from the brake van at the rear of his train. With two under each arm he hurried back to his engine, now underneath the roof of one of the troop train carriages.

Wallace managed to hoist his extinguishers up to this carriage roof and from this vantage point discharged them one after the other through the smoke. Sadly the streams of white foam had little effect for by this time the fire had such a grip that the flames soon blazed up again as strong as before.

Meanwhile the Mackie brothers raced back to Aithchison's Bank farm to collect an extinguisher and also a stirrup pump, speeding back on the farm motorcycle, bouncing across the fields. Yet although they soon had the stirrup pump working it, also had little effect on the inferno.

So John Mackie returned to the farm again, this time with David Wallace and a couple of soldiers, to collect the farm's force pump, which they rigged on a handcart and had working by about 7.30 am, some forty minutes after the accident.

With this they managed to draw some water from the ditch at the foot of the embankment. Though it was not much, they reckoned that the pump did save some lives because it delayed the advance of the flames allowing at least one knot of trapped soldiers to be rescued.

Nevertheless the pump was not without hazard for so densely packed was the wreckage that the confined space in which the unfortunate soldiers were trapped soon filled with water. A moment before they had been in imminent danger of being burnt to death; now they had to cry out to their rescuers to desist with the pump for fear of being drowned in the rising water.

Still, beside the power of the murderous conflagration, the farm force pump proved a puny instrument. Where, John Mackie asked, were the fire brigade? Despite three-quarters of an hour having passed since the collisions there was still no sign of them. John Mackie thought that he ought to set off again on his motorcycle to Carlisle to investigate..

On the engine of the goods train waiting in the down loop, driver Moss and Fireman Watson heard the troop train approaching and remembered seeing the signals lying off for it. They had seen the troop train pass them and had heard its brakes go on as the footplate crew had caught sight of the *Parly* standing on the line. They remembered the collision as a sustained and terrifying roar and remembered also the debris piling up around. Moss didn't think any of it had touched his train as it seemed to him to be lying mostly over towards the signal box.

Moss and Watson had climbed down from their cab to walk the couple of hundred yards back to the wreckage when the express ploughed into it, throwing some of the debris this time on to his goods train, the shock of which sheared a coupling, cutting their train in two and propelling the whole front half of his train forward by four or five yards.

Watson was to report later that he saw his own train on fire near to where the leading engine of the express had come off the rails and was leaning against some of his wagons that contained barrels. So Watson then went back to his engine to fetch a bucket of water which he threw on the flames. It was a singularly futile gesture, for the barrels in the wagons, which seemed to contain some combustible substance, were already alight.

To prevent the fire spreading up the train Watson uncoupled the burning wagons and then signalled to Moss to pull the train forward. In this way Moss was able to draw 33 undamaged wagons away from the developing inferno and out of the loop to safety on the down main line.

Reversing his train back down the main line Moss then ran the engine back up the loop coming to rest with his tender close to the fire around the derailed engines of the express. From here, he and Watson drew buckets of water from the engine's tender and threw them on the blaze, but they had virtually no effect at all. By now also the burning barrels still in the wagons in the loop were emitting a thick, black, choking smoke and the heat and the smoke together forced Moss and Watson to desist.

On the train engine of the express Driver Andrew Johnstone escaped from the collision without injury. His Fireman, John Graham, suffered a cut eye and bruises from a fall of coal but otherwise he too was little scathed. Their first thought was for their colleagues on the leading engine, which had taken the brunt of the impact.

Fireman Todhunter had struggled free from the coal that had engulfed him to the waist and all three footplatemen worked to save John Cowper pinned by coal against the hot wall of the firebox. As they worked they could feel of the fire in the wreckage around them and knew that they had only minutes before the coal that they were shifting with their bare hand caught light too.

In the event it took them nearly twenty minutes to free Cowper and then they carried him down to the field beside the line. He remained conscious throughout, though he had been badly burned about the neck and his whole body had been bruised by the avalanche of coal. Seeing his injuries, Andrew Johnstone made his way to the signal box to ensure that medical assistance was on its way. They could also use some tool vans, he thought.

With John Cowper saved, David Todhunter returned to his engine and shut off the injector that fed water to the boiler. It would be a long time before the train engine, number 48 in the Caledonian Railway's lists, would move again under her own steam.

Having been told in the signal box that medical assistance was indeed on its way, Fireman Andrew Johnstone returned to his engine. The fire around the two engines of the express was blazing quite out of control and already the paint had burnt off the tender of his engine, leaving the side curiously white and the metal far too hot to touch.

Johnstone remembered the steam driven hose used to keep down dust on the tender coals and clambered back on to the hot footplate to reach it, praying that it would still work.

As he turned the key there came the familiar rush of steam to the pump and moments later water gushed from the nozzle. Johnstone climbed on the tender and shielding his face with his arm against the fierce heat, which he could feel even through his clothes, played the hose into the middle of the smoke and flames. The water sent up great clouds of ash and and steam which left him half-choked, but peering into the smoke he couldn't see otherwise much evidence of an effect.

But then the force of a sudden explosion knocked Andrew Johnstone backwards and he fell off the tender, landing on the line some ten feet below. Bruised and battered, but luckily with no broken bones, he hauled himself to his feet again, and doggedly climbed back on the tender, throwing more water on the flames from a bucket. Again his efforts had negligible effect and so he abandoned them and went to rest by the lineside. His hands and face were scorched by the fire. "I was rather done-up." he said, afterwards.

Most likely it was the force of a gas cylinder exploding that threw him off the tender and might possibly have killed him. People later reported shards of metal shooting into the air and landing uncomfortably close to where the wounded were being tended in the fields beside the line. Charged to a pressure of eight atmospheres these cylinders were the reservoirs that supplied gas to the lights in the trains. They had been filled at Larbert ready for the journey south and as the fire took hold around them the pressure of the gas increased until eventually they burst, adding their inflammable contents to the conflagration.

SIXTEEN

As the able bodied helped the injured out of the wreckage and laid them out in the fields beside the line, the birds were singing beside the blackthorn hedges with their May blossom, or so people reported. Nor did the young burnt and injured soldiers of the Royal Scots disturb them much for most remained quietly and stoical and showed great spirit. They asked only for cigarettes, and perhaps a glass of water to relieve their pain, urging their rescuers, meanwhile, to get back to the train to save their friends. The teenage soldiers joked about their injuries with childish pride.

One such, lying out in the field with two broken legs, jested that he had been so badly mangled that had he had a third leg that would have been smashed too. Their one real regret however lay in knowing that they had suffered and died like this without having had the chance of facing an enemy and without the opportunity of giving a good account of themselves.

More men and women from the villages of Springfield and Gretna and from the surrounding countryside started to arrive bringing with them mattresses, sheets, cotton wool and bandages for the injured soldiers whom they laid out in the fields on cushions and bunks salvaged from the undamaged coaches of the express.

Among these helpers was Andrew Sword's wife who brought a supply of cotton for dressings with which she set to work. Later she reported that she would never forget the terrible sights of young men with such ghastly injuries and burns.

Mrs Burnett, who lived near the Meakins in Springfield also arrived promptly on the scene bringing with her a sheet and two of her husband's pocket handkerchiefs. With these she approached one soldier his face streaming with blood, but he brushed her aside: 'Oh it's all right - wait until we get the train cleared first.' But Mrs Burnett was not to be put off, insisting that the soldier would be better able to help others if she staunched the loss of blood and eventually the soldier agreed.

The splintering woodwork had caused many such lacerations - deep wounds that needed quick binding. A battalion travelling to war naturally carries with it a supply of field dressings - but the carnage at Gretna demanded many more than could be found in the trucks at the rear of the troop train. This supply soon ran out and so the soldiers' own puttees had to be unwound and pressed into service as makeshift bandages.

Inevitably many wounds proved too severe for first aid and as the day wore on more and more of the rescued soldiers succumbed to their injuries. These, with others who had been brought dead out of the troop train, now began one last journey to a barn attached to the nearby Quintinshill cottages, which had been pressed into service as a morgue. There their colleagues laid them out on the ground. The line of bodies grew steadily throughout the morning.

And still more men waited to be rescued or struggled to fight their way out of the train. Sergeant Fleeting, the veteran of the South African wars, had had charge of a platoon of soldiers in one of the compartments of the troop train that collapsed in the wreck, entombing the soldiers inside.

As the soldiers struggled to find a way through the wreckage they saw the splintered woodwork of the carriage now beginning to burn in the flames of the gas lights. Some of the soldiers panicked and Sergeant Fleeting had to roar and curse at them to restore discipline. Their determined efforts eventually discovered a way out through which the soldiers could wriggle one by one. Fleeting insisted that the injured should be got out first and then the able-bodied. He himself remained behind until all his men were out, shielding them from the flames with his back. Only then did he make his way out. His discipline had saved the lives of his men, but at some cost to himself for by the time he got clear his face and the upper part of his body had been badly burnt.

'Thank God,' one of them said later, 'we got clear of yon hell.'

But once free of the wreck these and other able-bodied soldiers showed great heroism in plunging back into the train again with picks and axes to rescue others. In a few cases this cost them their lives; in others they received terrible burns. But, directed by their officers, the work of rescue continued unceasingly.

Some said that the rescuers hacked away at the burning coaches as if storming a trench. forcing a way through the carriage roofs and hauling their comrades to safety. They worked, said an eye-witness 'in that silent, savage way of the Scots.'

Yet while many soldiers had to be hauled to safety at least one young man had an altogether different experience. He had had the presence of mind to raise his legs as the carriage telescoped and the bench seats of the compartment banged together. The roof of the compartment sheered off and the soldier found himself ejected from the carriage to land on the embankment beside the line, the horse hair cushion from the compartment still beneath him. Though the fall had knocked the wind out of him, the soldier was otherwise quite uninjured.

Meanwhile, in their compartment, Company Sergeant Major Simpson and Quartermaster Sergeant Donald Campbell had, with Bandmaster John Scott, been asleep at the time of the collision. Their carriage had telescoped, then lifted into the air to fall on its side. When movement stopped Scott could see Simpson's contorted figure. 'My arm's gone,' hissed the Sergeant Major through teeth clenched in pain. He had a serious head wound as well.

Seeing sky above him Bandmaster Scott climbed up through the wreck to seek help. He saw Simpson trying to follow, despite his injuries, helped by Donald Campbell. All three could smell smoke now, so Scott returned and lifted the Sergeant Major on his back and like this carried him out of the wrecked carriage which he could see lay against one of the empty coal wagons. They looked down into this and there in the bottom lay another sergeant, Sergeant Kean, pitched there in the collision and with both legs badly broken and wincing with pain.

Campbell and Scott managed to get Sergeant Major Simpson into the lineside field and the two men were about to return then for Sergeant Kean, when Simpson called back to them pointing with his one functional arm.

They looked and saw a young soldier whose head had been struck off in the collision and who now hung by his clothes on the wreckage, blood flowing in rivers down his khaki tunic. Campbell later retrieved the body, lifting the man down, but refusing to look at his identity disc, because, as he said, 'I have no wish to have to tell his folks.'

By now fire was raging along practically the entire length of the troop train wreckage and when soon it spread to the forward carriages of the express, rescuers were confronted by a wall of flame a hundred yards long.

Above the snap and spit of burning wood, and the occasional blast of a gas cylinder now came the staccato crack of exploding revolver ammunition.

Yet even in this inferno lay islands which the fire had not yet touched and from these came the desperate cries of young soldiers for rescue. But for most, trapped beyond reach, rescue was impossible, and their high-pitched screams as the fire engulfed them were thought by those who heard them to be far more affecting than any of the sights they saw that awful day.

In their desperation, soldiers trapped by an arm or leg called for saws or axes to sever their limbs and so escape the agony of being burnt alive. The first doctors to arrive at Quintinshill performed a number of rapid amputations under great pressure and danger to themselves and several soldiers owed their lives to the sacrifice of a limb.

A young soldier whose leg had been amputated to free him from the wreck in this way agreed that he was considerably luckier than some and even a man whose hands were amputated while the flames were licking his face believed himself better off than a poor man he had seen caught between the wagons of the goods train and the burning carriages of the London express and enveloped in a sheet of flame.

SEVENTEEN

Some, trapped beyond hope of rescue, seemed resigned to their awful fate. Three-quarters buried under an immense pile of wreckage into which the flames were already making inroads, lay eighteen year old Leo Kerr, the youngest of the three Kerr brothers on the train. Perhaps he knew that his case was hopeless, or that his body had been mortally smashed, for he motioned his rescuers away with a flick of his tired eyes, saying 'Don't mind me just now, there are others worse along the train.' So the rescuers moved on and in a few minutes the flames had closed around him. No further trace of Private Leo Kerr, the boy soldier from Leith, was ever found.

So intense was the fire that it drove back all but the most intrepid of the rescuers and some of these became badly burnt themselves and at least one man, uninjured in the collision, perished in trying to save the lives of others.

He was a naval officer, said witnesses later, who had organised the work of the naval ratings travelling in the rear of the express and who was last seen on the roof of a blazing carriage hacking away at it with a pick. But then the carriage lurched as the fire ate away at the wreckage and pitched the naval officer forward and down into the flames.

In some accounts his name is given as Commander Oliphant RN, but no such person appears in the casualty lists, although it is generally acknowledged that these were never totally accurate. The names of two other naval officers, however, do appear and these were Commander Head and Assistant Paymaster William Paton who had travelled together in the express. It is possible that the heroic naval officer may have been one of these.

Another casualty of the rescue was Private Charles Macdonald, the Musselburgh miner. Little the worse after the collision he at once set about assisting his friends, among them his travelling companion, William Williamson from Fisherrow. For an hour Macdonald struggled to remove the heavy carriage timbers beneath which Williamson lay trapped and unconscious as the flames edged nearer. But Macdonald kept at his work until the fire had scorched his face and head and hands. In this race for the body of the senseless William Williamson the flames won. Macdonald shielded his face with his hands but then collapsed himself, exhausted by the heat and the smoke and his burns. Luckily someone pulled him to safety.

The great bravery and disregard for their own injuries shown by the rescuers is evidenced by many tales of heroism. In the collision Private Creighton, another young Leith soldier, had been badly cut about hands and face by flying window glass. Witnesses reported blood pouring from his wounds as he charged at the debris in search of his friends.

Willie Elder, another Leith boy, climbed on the roof of a telescoped carriage, oblivious to the heat and the smoke, while Corporal Maloney crawled under the red hot tender of one of the locomotives and with his uniform scorched and smouldering, crawled out again dragging a living man. Michael O'Neill, a miner from Portobello, worked furiously for an hour and a half before being badly burnt trying to rescue another man trapped under one of the engines. He had rescued eight trapped men and got them to safety, but this ninth man proved too badly trapped and, like William Williamson, the flames took him.

Most of the Musselburgh men in Corporal Somerville's compartment had been asleep at the time of the collision, but James Arnott and his friend Arthur Colville, the gasman, had woken a few minutes earlier and were now enjoying their first cigarette of the day. Then came the initial collision, their coach cantered over and crumpled, and they found themselves pitched to the floor with the other six men in the compartment sprawled on top of them.

But just as the men were beginning to orient themselves and search for a way out, the leading engine of the London express hit their coach, sweeping it up and casting it aside in fragments. The floor gave way and, at the bottom of the pile of soldiers, Arnott and Colville found themselves tumbled down in a dark tomb of debris on to the sleepers of the railway track below.

Only bruised, Colville set about helping his friend whose leg seemed to be fractured. All around them they could hear their comrades, screaming and moaning in the burning wreckage. Then they, too, smelt the fire: the acrid pungent odour of burning horsehair and coach varnish, heard the crackle of the tinder-dry matchwood spitting and crackling, and they felt its heat. Then they saw flames just beyond the edge of the tomb of debris from which there appeared no exit.

Their cries for assistance went unaided. They might have been a hundred yards under the ground. Resigned to their fate, Colville suggested they pray for a quick death and being already on his knees he cried out for salvation. Arnott did likewise, both men choking on the suffocating smoke. They tore off their tunics, stuffing them down on the flames, in the vain hope of keeping the fire at bay a few moments longer.

Of the two Arnott was trapped closer to the flames to which the men's flimsy tunics presented no obstacle and despite his broken leg he reared up as the fire reached him, searing his back. To his great surprise this action caused his head to dislodge a loose piece of debris and he beyond he saw blue sky and the face of two sailors who grabbed hold of him and dragged him to safety. They returned immediately for Colville but by then the rush of air had charged the flames and the fire had closed around the pocket. Arthur Colville, the Musselburgh gasman, was another of whom no further trace was ever to be found.

Many would have preferred a bullet to being roasted alive and some indeed were crying out to their would be rescuers to shoot them. Kit Johnson, a rescuer who had hurried over from Springfield when news of the disaster reached him, found one soldier lying pinned by the wreckage and apparently lifeless. He was moving on when the soldier opened his eyes and implored Johnson to 'bring a rifle and shoot me.' But the soldier wasn't shot and Johnson believed his life was later saved, though the lower part of his legs had been reduced to charred stumps.

He wasn't the only one to call for a quick end: rescuers reported seeing a score of soldiers or their poor contorted bodies, scorched and charred by the flames lying towards the centre of the burning train. and some of these were crying out for a speedy despatch. John Mackie described these later as 'the most terrible cases' for the intense heat of the fire drove back successive waves of rescuers. No one could tell how many there were or how many had already died. They seemed to be piled up on each other and intermingled with debris and a number of observers reported afterwards that they had seen this 'great heap of bodies' lying under the carriages.

An officer then drew his pistol and advancing as far as the fire would let him emptied the chamber into pile of bodies. Beside the roaring of the fire and the screams and cries of the dying men, the service revolver did not sound very loud. The screams ceased then, but whether it was from fire or bullet none could tell.

By this time the fire had reached the rear of the train and blazing so fiercely with sparks flying all around that the safety of the battalion's stores and ammunition trucks could not be guaranteed despite their earlier separation from the carriages of the train. Captain Romanes therefore ordered soldiers to remove the ammunition carts from the truck closest to the fire. They removed two carts to safety but the third stuck fast and from this boxes of ammunition had to be carried out.

Quartermaster Sergeant Donald Campbell, still in his stockinged feet, volunteered for this work and he was to say later that it had been a most trying time for the fire made the danger of an explosion very real. He had been very thankful when all the ammunition had been removed and he could rest in safety.

EIGHTEEN

Those Scottish soldiers and sailors travelling home on leave in the London express who were awake might well have let out a cheer as their train crossed the Border and headed into Scotland. But the men of the Royal Field Artillery travelling with Private James Richardson were cautious: 'We are damned near there,' said one. 'But we'd better not crow until we're home.' The advice was prophetic.

Richardson went outside into the corridor and at that moment the express ran into the wreckage of the troop train and the roof burst off the carriage. Richardson remembered how he had been shot up through space as the carriage telescoped and had landed on the embankment beside the line, temporarily losing consciousness in the fall. But he hadn't been badly injured and afterwards was able to help with the rescue.

In sleeping car 5132 Lieutenant Kirksop woke somewhere between Carlisle and Gretna to ask Lieutenant Bonnar the time. Bonnar fumbled for his watch and it was at that precise moment that Bonnar died with the time of the accident on his lips. The elegant twelve wheeled sleeping car began to telescope, the floor of the compartment gave way and Kirsop found himself precipitated out of his bunk and on to the railway line below.

The collapsing wreckage pinned his legs, though fortunately he had fallen between two mattresses that cushioned his fall and protected his legs from injury. Despite this he felt the weight of the wreckage on top of him. All seemed quiet, with no fire or explosion nearby. Of Lieutenant Bonnar there appeared no sign.

Thus Kirksop lay buried in the wreckage for what he thought was half an hour or so, then he caught the smell of drifting smoke and renewed his efforts to attract attention. At last someone hacked through the carriage roof and lowered a loop of rope, with which, when he had fastened it around him, he was hauled to safety. Somebody then quickly threw a blanket around him: having been asleep at the time of the accident Kirksop was, in his own words, 'very scantily clad.'

Despite the protection of the mattresses, his back and legs were severely bruised and the rescuers laid him out in the field beside the line where a doctor gave him morphine to ease the pain. Lying there he marvelled at the contrast between the fury of the burning train and the screams of the dying and the idyllic May morning, the sun climbing into a blue sky across which floated fluffy white clouds, the lush dewey green of the grass fields and the pink and white blossom of the hedgerows.

For his part, Richard Levanowski, the sleeping car attendant had been making early morning tea at the time of the collision which had thrown him against the front wall of his pantry. Fortunately he was uninjured and so could make his way forward to see that sleeping car 5132 had been shunted backwards into his own coach. In the wreckage a young officer lay unconscious. Some sailors came up at this point from the rear of the train and together they managed to free him.

Below they found Mr Macdonald and his wife who had occupied the rearmost berth of 5132 and out of the comfort of which the collision had precipitated him, like Kirksop, on to the railway line below. Mrs Macdonald would have followed too had she not managed to cling to her bunk, shouting for help.

She, too. was heard eventually by the ubiquitous Quartermaster-Sergeant Campbell who picked her up and carried her in his arms down to the field below. Apart from a bang to the knee she appeared to be unscathed.

Her husband had not the same fortune for considerable debris had fallen on top of him. By the time Campbell and Levanowski reached him the coach was on fire and in their haste to get him out let a heavy piece of iron fall on his hand, crushing two of his fingers. However, his life was saved. Yet Macdonald's recorded thoughts did not focus on his rescue from the conflagration, but rather on whether he might ever be able to play golf again.

Mr Terryer and his wife had been dozing in an ordinary compartment at the time of the crash. He said afterwards that the coach had buckled like a concertina, the roof splitting open and the seat of the carriage lifting right up into the air. The next moment he found himself on the remains of the carriage roof from where he was pitched on to the embankment as the carriage tilted over. Uninjured he heard his wife calling from inside the wreck. Summoning the assistance of a soldier Terryer managed to get her out of the wreck. Apart from a bump to the head, she, too, had not been injured and the lucky Terryers were able to continue their journey to Glasgow later in the day.

Nearby, another couple, whose names have not come down to us, had a similarly spectacular escape. As the compartment had collapsed they had both fallen between the seats and now lay pinned by the wreckage side by side. But he had fallen with his arm across her throat. Two pieces of timber pinned it there and his efforts to free his arm only resulted in increased pressure on his wife's throat. He could see he was involuntarily strangling her and worse, that they would soon be engulfed by the flames. His desperate shouts for help went unanswered while his wife's face was becoming dangerously black. The heat became intense and it seemed their clothing would soon catch fire. But just when it seemed that all was lost a group of sailors broke through and extricated them both in the nick of time.

Others in the train were not so lucky. Of the three officers that had been selected for a few precious days' leave from the bloody battles of Flanders, only Lieutenant Kirksop survived. Lieutenant Bonnar simply disappeared, his body consumed utterly by the flames. Captain Finlay also died in the train, his body badly burnt. So too perished Herbert Ford, the manager of the crane works and Lieutenant Jackson, who would finally now be free forever from rheumatism.

The Newcastle draper, Mr Nimmo, escaped injury, but his young wife and baby died. She had gone forward with the baby shortly before the crash and now, having escaped the wreck Nimmo watched the train on fire and saw the charred body of a woman with a baby still clutched in her arms lying in the wreck. That he had escaped himself seemed almost a curse.

Samuel Dyer, the attendant in charge of saloon 5132 had just collected the tea cups from the berth occupied by William Mackenzie, the refrigerating engineer, and his wife. They told reporters afterwards that everything in their compartment had seemed to collapse and the luggage had come tumbling out of the racks. However neither were seriously injured.

Afterwards Mackenzie could only remember the tremendous heaps of debris and the fire and the terrible screaming that seemed to be all around, exacerbated by the roar of escaping steam from the engines. He and his wife then searched for Samuel Dyer but they could find no trace of the attendant. He, like so many others, had perished and this made the Mackenzies sad. 'He had been so kind to us with the tea,' said Mrs Mackenzie.

A light north-easterly breeze fanned the flames towards the carriages of the express and on it a pall of black smoke rose into the bright blue sky. Cushioned by the telescoping coaches in front of them, the rear coaches had been left relatively undamaged, their passengers able to scramble down upon the line with little more than the occasional bruise.

Many of these were able to help with the rescue. Private Duncan Gordon had spent seven months in the Flanders trenches with the 2nd Gordon Highlanders before being granted leave. He had vivid memories of the recent battle for Neuve Chapelle with its 12,000 casualties, its trench shambles and hospital suffering, but he admitted shedding a tear when he saw the plight of the Royal Scots at Gretna. There was, he thought, a painful contrast between slaughter with a purpose on the battlefield and death in your own homeland in an avoidable accident.

Even Robert Bain and his two motor transport driver colleagues, who had boarded the crowded Glasgow express at Euston but then left it to take the train from St Pancras, turned up by car at Quintinshill, having heard about the accident at Carlisle. There they spent all day helping the injured and thanking their stars that they had missed the express. Robert Bain felt that never in his life had he seen such harrowing scenes which he never would be able to erase from his memory.

NINETEEN

Despite there being a direct telephone link between the Quintinshill cabin and Carlisle it was not until 7.15, some twenty-five minutes after the collision of the troop train with the *Parly,* that District Superintendent Blackstock heard about the accident while eating breakfast at his house in Carlisle. He reacted expeditiously, making various calls to the civil authorities and telling John Campbell, the stationmaster at Carlisle Citadel station to prepare a special train to bring up emergency assistance.

By the time Blackstock reached his office in the Citadel station the train was waiting. So too were four doctors (Drs Lediard, Crawford-Aitkin, Helm and Balfour-Paul) as well as nurses and ambulance men, sent down from the infirmary, all asking why they had been so rapidly summoned this early in the morning. Rumour had it that a London express had crashed on the Border, but no-one had any details. Despite the telephone link certainly no-one there appreciated the scale of the disaster.

Instead the emergency train consisting of two carriages and a brake van had been loaded with a miscellany of what the stationmaster thought might be required: a dozen fire extinguishers, a dozen fire buckets, two fifty foot lengths of fire hose and a quantity of ambulance boxes, a dozen stretchers. Ten minutes later, at 7.45, almost an hour after the accident, it steamed out of the station for the twenty minute journey to Quintinshill.

The train drew up behind the undamaged coaches of the express and the medical crew climbed down to the tracks. By now the conflagration was out of control along a front of a hundred yards and enveloping the goods trains in the loop lines as well as the three wrecked trains on the running lines. A vast pall of black smoke climbed from this holocaust into a bright blue sky and the heat could be felt some distance away.

In the fields, scattered all around, lay hundreds of dead and dying men, women and children - some with horrifying injuries - and they cried out for pain relief. Blackstock must have realised at once the inadequacy of his supplies for he went immediately to the signal cabin to telephone for more assistance. What good were a dozen stretchers when already forty lifeless bodies had been taken out of the wreck and laid in the whitewashed Quintinshill steading and the number of seriously injured seemed almost uncountable. And what use could the dozen fire extinguishers possibly be against an inferno one hundred yards long and ten yards wide?

The four doctors went to work immediately among the wounded. They could not guess at what had happened or at what trains might have been involved. A fierce battle might have taken place, they said afterwards, with dead and wounded scattered in all directions. Someone had cut away the wire fencing to the railway and now down the embankment the ambulance men carried a further stream of bodies, some living, some dead and some grotesquely mutilated.

They brought them down to the eastern side of the line, where the blossoming hawthorn hedges enclosed the pasture field. Experienced soldiers returning from the terrors of the Flanders trenches believed the scene to be ten times worse than anything they had experienced before. The stone floor of the white-washed Quintinshill steading, pressed into service as a morgue, soon became covered with a pitiful carpet of the dead.

A handful of local doctors summoned by urgent calls from the Gretna Post Office had arrived before the emergency train. Others, unable to make the emergency train motored directly from their homes in and around Carlisle. Among these was a young rugby playing surgeon, Dr Edwards, who raced the train in his car and beat it to Quintinshill.

Another was Dr Taylor from Longtown who had already been out all night attending to a patient with a critical illness. He had been driving home in the early morning when he'd heard the sound of the collision, the noise of which he said was like a loud clap of thunder some way off.

Red-eyed from lack of sleep, Dr Taylor noted that many bodies taken out of the troop train had been horribly scorched. He looked at the the wreckage and the fire and heard the cries of the men trapped inside and guessed there would be many more bodies carried to the Quintinshill steading before the day was out.

He reckoned he saw pretty much every kind of injury that day from the relatively straightforward broken arms, legs, collar bones and ribs to the far more serious cases where soldiers had spinal injuries, or had been crushed, or lacerated deeply by woodwork splinters from the collapsing train. In addition many men were also concussed.

But the worst cases, he said, were undoubtedly those who had been caught by the fire or by escaping steam and had clothes, skin or even flesh burnt from a limb and who were in great pain. And here the problem was not at first a lack of morphia, but simply a lack of water in which to dissolved the tablets. 'The fire was dreadful,' said Dr Taylor afterwards with a shudder, remembering the carriages flaring like matches.

Many soldiers were taken out of the wreck with limbs that required urgent amputation. These operations were performed behind makeshift barriers, or sometimes behind no barrier at all. Soldiers put out by chloroform would wake up to see their amputated limbs lying on the grass

112

beside them, there being no time otherwise to dispose of them.

Dr Denny, another local doctor who hurried to the scene, recalled that for the most part the Royal Scots showed great bravery. He heard only one or two moaning in agony: one of these had suffered an internal injury; the other a fractured spine. Those with broken arms or legs scarcely complained at all, he said.

One soldier - 'a brave little fellow, a fine chap he was' - whose toes had been burned off and both of whose legs were broken, had waved Dr Denny away, pointing to others with even more serious injuries. 'I'm all right,' he said. 'All I want is a cigarette.'

He recalled another soldier whose legs had also been crushed and burned and who was in a semi-delirious state. Nevertheless, he tried to smile as Denny approached and implored the doctor to 'hurry up and remove the horse that has been sitting on my legs for the past hour.'

TWENTY

Many owed their lives to the prompt and selfless actions of the doctors who worked in some cases for a full twenty-four hours without a break, first at the line side and then after in the Carlisle hospitals to which the men were taken where emergency operations continued until 3 am the next morning.

Nowhere was this selfless spirit better shown than where the doctors managed to extract living soldiers from the burning train, often by a hurried amputation of their imprisoned limbs. In the process their suits of fine tweed soon became as charred as the burnt and tattered tunics of the Royal Scots. Two doctors in particular - Dr Warwick from Gretna and the rugby playing surgeon, Dr Edwards from Carlisle, performed particularly heroic feats crawling beneath the burning wreckage to ease the suffering of one man after another.

For anyone found alive there came first an injection of morphine, then an amputation if that were necessary. Duncan Gordon, the Neuve Chapelle veteran from the express, attached himself to Dr Edwards and held down several soldiers while he amputated their limbs.

Frequently soldiers had been caught and held by their feet as the coaches telescoped and the seats banged together and sometimes the feet were so crushed that they had to be amputated with the boots still on them.

Dr Sheehan, an Irish doctor from Carlisle, was another active in the search for survivors. Crawling beneath the wagons of the goods train, in a pocket the fire had not yet reached, he came across a pile of bodies, most dead but some still alive and all lying in one confused heap. Amongst them Sheehan was alarmed to see two large gas cylinders.

It was nearly 10 o'clock and the fire was reaching its zenith and closing fast around the pocket on three sides. Nevertheless, Sheehan thought that he might be able to rescue two of the soldiers and so summoned assistance. Railwaymen and soldiers levered away at the wreckage while someone played bursts of water from the force pump on the encroaching flames.

They got the first man out without too much difficulty and then the rescuers went back for the second. He lay underneath two dead men and though still alive himself this man's leg was hopelessly trapped and would need to be severed. The fire in any case was now beginning to lick at his feet. 'But he was a brave fellow,' said Dr Sheehan afterwards, 'for he never murmured.'

'Just lie there still for a minute or two and we'll have you out all right,' said the doctor. 'Well try not to be too long about it, I am getting pretty fed up,' returned the soldier calmly.

Sheehan called for a surgeon and Dr Edwards came with his knives and a borrowed carpenter's saw. Together they crawled beneath the wagons while others began tying a tourniquet around the trapped leg. By now the flames were beginning to lick at the large gas cylinders so they worked speedily, so speedily in fact that the tourniquet had been tightened before the realisation struck that it was on the wrong leg. Sheehan meanwhile was preparing a chloroform mask but so many sparks floated in the air that the mask ignited before it could be applied. A second mask then had to be prepared outside the pocket and this was used successfully.

The actual amputation took but thirty seconds to cut the flesh and saw through the thigh bone, Dr Edwards slashing away the trouser leg and the flesh in one quick incision. Willing hands then dragged the unconscious soldier to safety where the flow of blood was staunched and the stump dressed. Sadly the delays with tourniquet and chloroform had let the fire reach the bottom of his remaining leg, which was burnt and charred.

This anonymous soldier, whose name no-one sought to report, was the last man to be taken alive out of the wreck. He had suffered terribly and despite the heroic attempts of the doctors and their helpers who had risked their own lives, he died an hour or two later.

Dr Edwards found himself in a state of collapse from the smoke and heat in the confined space and he took a little time to recover. But later he tried to play down his part in the rescue saying that it had all been a team effort which would not have been possible without Dr Sheehan, and he went on to speak of the cool, raw courage of the Royal Scots.

'What really impressed me,' he said, 'was the way they behaved. They really were quite magnificent. There was no grumbling and the fellows who were injured and could not get loose stuck it out splendidly.'

He confessed they were all very nervous during the last operation for all knew only too well the danger they faced from the two gas cylinders that might have exploded at any time. He also recalled exploding revolver ammunition, 'It was bad for the nerves.' he said.

By now more rescuers had arrived at the scene and some of the more seriously injured could be removed to hospitals in Carlisle. Carried by their less seriously injured colleagues, fifty-two men were laid out in the undamaged coaches of the express and in these, coupled to the engine of the emergency train, they were taken back to Carlisle.

Private Archibald Gilchrist of the Scots Guards who had been a passenger on the express found himself in charge of five of the injured men. One of these he reported later had been horribly mangled. Some time before the train reached Carlisle this man took Gilchrist's hand and said in a low and husky voice, 'You have done your best,' and gave up the ghost.

TWENTY-ONE

One of the curious matters about the accident was the time it took for the various authorities to react, despite a working telephone link between the Quintinshill signal cabin and Carlisle.

It took nearly an hour to despatch a special relief train and a further twenty minutes for it to arrive. When it did, Chief Superintendent Blackstock went to the signal cabin and spent a great deal of time telephoning. Far from taking steps to mitigate the disaster, however, his primary interest seems to have been in managing the interruption to the Caledonian schedules and arranging diversions for the trains. No one thought to mention the accident to the civil authorities and when they did the message was not relayed via a telegram or call from senior railway official like Blackstock but instead came via a breathless and anonymous sailor who turned up at the Central Police Station at Carlisle, almost two hours after the collision, with the news that there had been a serious railway accident near Gretna and could they please summon out the fire brigade as many people had been killed and injured and the crashed trains were ablaze.

Although quite likely incredulous, the duty inspector at the Police Station nevertheless had the sense promptly to relay this intelligence by telephone to Eric Herbert de Schmid, the Chief Constable of Carlisle who doubled as the Director of the City's Fire Brigade. Being the weekend de Schmid received the message at his home.

In view of the serious fires that had followed other recent railway accidents, it is difficult to understand de Schmid's tardy reaction. Only two years before, at Ais Gill, only twenty miles from Carlisle, fourteen people had been burnt to death when their gas-lit train collided with one that was following. De Schmid would have known this and must have known that every minute counted when it came to saving lives.

But instead of acting he merely told the inspector who had called him that he could not send out the fire brigade without further information, although in anticipation he would meanwhile ask the brigade to stand by. He then put though a call to the Citadel station.

In Superintendent Blackstock's absence, de Schmid's call was taken by the Chief Clerk who remarked 'we know very little about it at present, Mr Chief, but I understand that the fire is out, and we may want the ambulance.' As the fire at the time was raging along a front of 100 yards and the number of dead and injured ran into the hundreds, this must rank as one of the most complacent statements of all time.

Maybe he remembered the dozen fire extinguishers and the two fifty foot lengths of hose that had gone up to Quintinshill on the special train and considered those would by now - two hours after the accident - have done their job.

In the various inquiries and inquests that followed the disaster, the failure to summon the emergency services immediately was never mentioned. No-one seems to have commented on this complacency or on the delays that occurred before the civil authorities became involved, or to have investigated how such delays might have arisen. Indeed, how the Chief Clerk at Carlisle Citadel station - just ten miles away from Quintinshill - not have known what was happening when telephone and telegraph links existed between the two?

A little while later another caller arrived at the police station, this time on a motorcycle. It was John Mackie, the farmer's son, who may have given a more authoritative account than the breathless sailor had done earlier for the duty inspector again called de Schmid who at last authorised the departure of the fire brigade. The little motor engine departed for Quintinshill at 8.55. By then the fire had been burning for two hours and the brigade were still ten miles away.

Even when the brigade finally arrived it took another hour to get their fire hoses into action for there simply was no adequate supply of water to be had at the site and the brigade had to run a hose to the river Sark half a mile to the south. There they set the engine and it was lucky that they had hose and power enough to pump the river water to the three branch jets at the end of the hose. The first gushes shot out of the end of the hose at around 10 am, just as the fire had reached its zenith, and as the last man pulled alive from the flaming wreckage. No more of the Royal Scots remained alive for the fire brigade to save.

Apart from sending clouds of steam and ash up into the air, the water from the fire hose had little effect, so fierce had the conflagration become. So great was the heat, and so extensive the quantity of combustible material lying about, that although the fire brigade pumped water continuously from 10 am until midnight, and intermittently thereafter, the fire only began to come under control when hardly anything remained unburnt.

But having come they were determined to do their duty and so the men of the Carlisle Fire Brigade worked at the sight, wet, burnt and weary, without a break for 24 hours, not returning home to Carlisle until nine o'clock next morning.

From the railways company, however, the response was anything but tardy or inadequate, though it suggested that the Caledonian cared more about its traffic than anything else. Almost before the last soldiers were taken out of the wreckage and long before the fire at Quintinshill had been put out, special trains were leaving Glasgow marshalled to included breakdown, repair and recovery equipment. Other emergency repair trains in Motherwell and Carlisle were also being sent on their way.

These trains also brought Sir Charles Bine-Renshaw, Chairman of the Caledonian; and a number senior Caledonian officials including Donald Matheson, General Manager, and Thomas Pettigrew, the General Superintendent of the Line and his assistant Robert Killin. All arrived in the late forenoon, while the fire was still blazing through the five trains, to assess the damage to the line and its consequences and to begin understanding what had happened.

Robert Killin cornered the signalmen Meakin and Tinsley in the signal box, but they were scarcely in a fit state to make rational statements. Tinsley admitted, however, to forgetting about the *Parly,* the local train that he had shunted on to the opposite running line.

After an initial investigation in which he checked that everything possible was being done for the wounded, the Caledonian Chairman left his officials to work out emergency timetables with the staff at the Citadel station and went to visit the wounded at the Cumberland Infirmary.

TWENTY-TWO

Soon after this, from north and south, the breakdown trains arrived with great steam cranes to clear away the wreckage so that new rails could be laid. The crews worked steadily all through that Saturday and then in the moonlight and under the glare of paraffin pressure lamps through the night that followed.

The fire brigade would play their hoses on the debris until it became cool enough for lifting gear to be attached and then the cranes would puff and rumble and a fragment of railway truck or carriage would be hauled up and pitched down the embankment off the line.

Piece by piece the great cranes would lift an obstruction out of the way; then the crane would retire and the platelayers would go in to lay new temporary rails to enable the crane to advance a few yards further into the wreckage.

Meanwhile, helpers and rescuers continued to arrive at the lineside. By the afternoon, as the steam cranes were grinding away, half-burnt clothing and blood-stained bandages littered the fields. The injured claimed temporary beds among the elegant couches and cushions taken out of the first class compartments of the express. And beside the tracks lay piles of recovered equipment, mostly damaged beyond repair. This included many rifles, now just twisted steel tubes of a pinkish-blue colour. But there were also personal belongings to be recovered.

Corporal Wood, the Musselburgh man, who had been the sole survivor of the seven who travelled in his compartment, was given the task of collecting such of these as might have survived the fire, and he put them together in sad little heaps beside the line. He found a rosary and a crucifix and put it in one pile with a cigarette case and a pocket book bearing the name of Kenneth J Campbell. He found Campbell's visiting cards, too, which bore the address 'Magdalen College.' Presumably Mr Campbell had been a passenger on the express.

In another pile he put French franc notes of varying values together with a case on which the name 'Alistair Stewart, 9th Argyll and Sutherland Highlanders' had been stamped in gold leaf; another passenger on the express, no doubt. The case had fallen open and as Wood gathered up the contents he noted a letter addressed to a lady in Edinburgh. This the corporal put into his pocket for posting later.

In yet another pile he put a silver-mounted dirk, with the initials D. McG scratched on the handle and letters to be delivered by hand in Dumbarton. These he laid on top of some charred greatcoats and the remains of ration provisions, much damaged by fire. He found a quantity of burnt soldiers boots, too, which he placed on the pile and then a single lady's shoe, quite clean and undamaged.

Another card case which Corporal Wood picked up contained a railway ticket and some calling cards. And on these was printed the name of Captain Robert Scott Finlay.

The Corporal was to remark afterwards on the number of books and magazines that seemed to be everywhere and which somehow had escaped the fire. One paper, which showed signs of having been held in some fierce grip had the name of W. Bailie printed upon it and next to this, quite melted by the fire, lay a large unopened box of chocolates out of which the contents had flowed out and over a bundle of regimental papers bearing a sealed tag reading *for use on board ship.'* A novel entitled *'The Day' or 'The Passing of a Throne'* lay open on the green grass beside them.

Towards four in the afternoon, six hours after the last man had been pulled alive from the wreck, Colonel Peebles decided that his men had done all they could and that no further purpose would be served by their remaining at Quintinshill. So he had them summoned for a roll call prior to embarking them on a train for Carlisle.

Nine hours had passed since the accident during which time all the uninjured soldiers had laboured heroically to save their friends. Now hungry, thirsty and physically exhausted after a disturbed night, they presented a sorry sight. If they themselves had escaped with their lives, they had lost their equipment and personal belongings. And many of their good friends had been burned alive.

Those left uninjured had first worked at the wreck and then in the fields beside the line, tending the wounded and carrying bodies to the makeshift mortuary in the nearby Quintinshill steading. Some had accompanied the most seriously injured on trains to Carlisle.

Captain Romanes, the battalion adjutant, his tunic torn and his face smeared with grease, blew a whistle to call the men to muster.

Under the shadow of the dark pall of smoke from the still burning wreckage, the soldiers drifted in, in ones and twos, to the field on the east side of the line where Sergeant Dutt, the only sergeant in the whole half battalion to have escaped injury, and who now wore a civilian cap instead of the Royal Scots Glengarry, ordered them into two thin lines.

A sympathetic crowd of spectators watched from a respectable distance. A small knot of officers stood at the front, their uniforms scorched and burnt. The surviving soldiers presented an even more pitiful sight, standing there exhausted in the afternoon sun, their faces blackened by smoke.

Although they kept their military bearing, the survivors looked more like the last remnant of a corps that had just come through some fearful battle, rather than an accident within their own homeland. They gazed around, bewildered, overcome by fatigue from nine hours of ceaseless and frantic labour. Peebles and Romanes looked around the field hoping they could see stragglers and Romanes gave another blast on his whistle for they could not believe that these two thin lines, which together could not amount to more than fifty men, were all that remained of the half battalion that had set out from Larbert that morning. Others could not believe it either and at least one officer turned away with tears in his eyes.

Even the battalion rolls had been lost to the fire, so no-one could actually say who had been on the troop train. Nevertheless, Colonel Peebles went along the line with Sergeant Dutt noting down the names. As they did this another four men came up and took their places so that when the list was complete there were 52 names upon it - from which, Colonel Peebles concluded, that almost ninety per cent of the 468 soldiers who had set out that morning had either been killed or were now casualties. More than four hundred young men had either died in the accident or in the fire that followed or else had suffered wounds that made them incapable of parading.

Of the 52 men left standing, only two came from 'A' company which had occupied the front half of the train. Apart from their officer, Captain Wightman, the battalion's entire signalling section had been wiped out.

The list finished Sergeant Dutt barked the order to 'stand easy,' and then in consideration of the men's physical condition told them they could lie down. One by one the officers followed suit and, as they lay on the grass, they said little to one another, feeling numb and shocked and exhausted. Instead they lay on their backs or propped up on their elbows watching the melancholy procession of stretcher bearers carrying the dead away from the railway line. Many of their burdens seemed horribly light.

Soon a train arrived and at last the uninjured Royal Scots of 'A' and 'D' companies were able to continue their journey to Carlisle.

TWENTY-THREE

By the late afternoon news of the disaster had broken widely. From Carlisle crowds of people set out on the ten mile journey to the site of the accident, some with a genuine desire to offer assistance but most simply to gawp at the spectacle. The roads about Gretna became thick with pedestrians and cyclists for this was still a fine Whit-Saturday weekend and a holiday for most people. On this crush the police tried to impose some order and to stop the wider public interfering with the salvage.

They must have had some success, too, for several reports of the disaster in the newspapers criticised the constabulary complaining that the policemen seemed to have nothing better to do than to stop newspapermen from earning a living.

Through these crowds during the late afternoon arrived a steady stream of coffins, raided from every undertaker in the locality. The special trains that came out from Glasgow and Carlisle carried coffins too and one by one the dead soldiers were placed reverently in them. The Quintinshill steading that had been used as a makeshift mortuary, had soon filled up and so the dead were being laid out under shrouds outside in the open air.

Many were burnt and mutilated and the coffin lids were screwed down quickly just as soon as the body could be identified from its dog tag. The coffins were then laid out in the sunshine in a long double line whose length never seemed to change for as newly filled coffins joined the line, others were taken away to be loaded on to trains to take them on their final journey.

Late in the day the salvage crews discovered the burnt remains of Frank Scott's body lying among the ashes on the footplate of No 121, the troop train engine. The body of Fireman James Hannah's body lay beside it. From what was left of the two men no-one could say whether they had been killed outright in the first collision or whether they had survived that and had died when the express had hit, or whether they had been trapped and died in the fire. But the probability was that they had been killed outright when their engine ran into the *Parly*.

But it was not until the following morning that the cranes were able to move No 121, which lay on her side at what had been the centre of the wreck. Her wheels had been warped by the fire and the gangers had great difficulty in putting her back on the rails again. The locomotive had suffered greatly in the collision, her cylinders, frame and driving gear had been bent and wrecked and the inspectors took the decision to cut her up immediately for scrap.

As for No 121's nemesis, the great Cardean locomotive that had drawn the *Parly*, the inspectors hoped that she could be saved for the wartime traffic was making great demands on the Caledonian's stock of heavy locomotives. Perhaps she could be rebuilt; they scratched their heads. But when Locomotive Superintendent Pickersgill examined her a few days later he quickly rejected this idea. Her boiler plates had been sprung and the collision had cracked her frame. There was no alternative: she would have to be cut up too. Pickersgill's only consolation was that he thought he could salvage the engines of the express.

Finally, on the Sunday morning, just over twenty-four hours after the accident, the breakdown crews finally had the lines clear of wreckage for the platelayers to go in and remove the temporary rails and in their place lay new, permanent track. At the same time they restored the paraphernalia of points and signals so that soon it was hard to tell what damage the accident had done.

In fact thirty-four rails had been twisted or broken by the collision or in the heat of the fire and thirty-five railway sleepers had burnt entirely away. A further one hundred and sixty five sleepers had been damaged along with their cast iron rail chairs that held the rails and secured them to the sleepers. Each of these weighed a half hundred weight and four hundred and fifty seven of them had been smashed as the trains derailed.

Despite all bodies having long since been removed from the wreck the platelaying gangs continued to find incinerated human remains. Sometime in the afternoon they came across a human foot - which, for quickness and simplicity, they buried in a hole beside the line, there being no way of telling to whom it might once have belonged.

With the new line laid, the wreckage tipped down the embankment was lifted again and put in trucks to be taken away, so that by the Monday morning a few wheels and axles and a broken couple of trucks were all that remained by the line. The spread of charred and blood-stained clothing and the litter of personal effects were also speedily removed, so the only evidence of the tragedy, which couldn't easily be effaced, were the thousands of footprints in the fields and the scorched paintwork on the Quintinshill signal cabin.

In the modern age we might expect a week, or even two, might elapse before a line would be open again after such an accident, but the Caledonian's lines had been cleared and relaid after Quintinshill by six o'clock on the Sunday evening and the gangers declared the work complete and finished less than 36 hours after the accident. Yet strangely, after all this furious activity on their part, no trains appeared in either direction for a full hour and a half.

George Meakin reported as usual for the Sunday night shift at the Quintinshill signal box. The accident, he reasoned, had not taken place on his shift. It was Tinsley who had forgotten about the *Parly* and pulled off the fatal signals. He could not see that any fault could attach to him and so he was taken aback to find another man in his box and to be told that he was himself suspended.

While he argued his case, however, a mail train left Edinburgh, bound for Carlisle and the south beyond and this train - the up *'Limited Mail'* - was the first to run over the new Quintinshill metals.

The telegraph rang in the Quintinshill cabin to tell the relief signalman that the Mail had passed Lockerbie. Now she was passing Kirtlebridge and now the box at Kirkpatrick-Fleming belled the train on. The signalman accepted the train and with only a momentary pause pulled over the levers that controlled the up distant and up home signals, the same levers that had been pulled by Tinsley just 36 hours before with such fatal consequences.

The semaphore arms crashed down and the signalman moved over to the window and looked toward the north-west. At first he saw nothing, his view obscured by the light from the low evening sun shining along the line. But he heard the rumble of a train and, seconds later, saw the mushroom of steam billowing around the granite overbridge.

The train came on. At moderate speed only for the new track had not yet been consolidated and the signalman watched as it curved its way past his cabin and on towards the south. It did not collide with any of the platelaying wagons still parked in the loop lines but ran on up the line without a problem and the signalman watched as it passed slowly out of sight behind the cutting and over the Border. Then the signalman returned all his signals to danger and entered the time in the train register book.

TWENTY-FOUR

Towards five on the Saturday afternoon the little train carrying all that remained of the half-battalion, the 52 out of the 468, reached Carlisle. From the Citadel station they marched through the cobbled streets to Carlisle Castle, the local barracks. News of the disaster had preceded them for folk now came out of their houses and lined the route. Now and again, someone let out an occasional cheer, but mostly the fatigue and horror etched into the soldiers' faces stunned the crowd into silence. As they marched along the soldiers chanted a dirge for their fallen comrades whose painful refrain rang out over the cobbles. *'We shall never, never, see them any more.'*

At this point these shattered troops were still under orders to proceed to Liverpool and sail to Gallipoli. Indeed the other half of the battalion were already at Liverpool. So it was not clear how long the Royal Scots would be staying at the Castle once they had eaten and rested. It appeared at first they would be moving on directly. This they were clearly in no fit state to do. So

Colonel Peebles agreed with the garrison commander that they should stay at the Castle for at least a couple of days to recuperate.

After he had seen that his men were at least temporarily in safe charge, Colonel Peebles retreated to the no doubt more comfortable accommodation of the County Hotel and there he began a flurry of correspondence - writing telegrams, requesting orders and reporting the day's events.

There also the press caught up with him. He said he had been deeply grieved by the accident, especially in view of the disastrous consequences it had had for the regiment. He recalled how splendidly officers and men had worked together throughout months of hard training since the outbreak of war the previous August. Officers and men, he said, had been on close terms and ready for any amount of hard work at the front, all looking forward with enthusiasm to doing their bit for their country. The accident had been a terrible tragedy; an unexpected sorrow.

For their part, in the Castle's mess some of the soldiers ate hungrily after their day's exertions, others pushed their plates away, unable to stomach food after the day long stench of their colleagues roasting in the flames of the wreckage. Feelings of nausea outweighed their appetites. They couldn't rest, either, for as soon as they lay down their heads would fill with harrowing images and they would hear again the distressed screaming of their friends.

It may have been a relief therefore when a sergeant called them to a medical parade in the evening twilight. The Castle's resident surgeon-major cursorily examined each one of them on the parade ground and, incredibly, declared them all fit.

Sir James Spencer Ewart, the commander of the King's armies in Scotland, saw them too, and no doubt also thought them fit. It was the second time he had seen these men for he had visited the accident earlier in the day and had come on to Carlisle. Passing the parade ground he asked his driver to stop, stood up and saluted them. The men stood to attention, their officers returning the salute. And then Sir James Spencer Ewart drove out of the Castle and into the dusk.

Colonel Peebles had now received a reply to his request for orders: the men were to collect new kit and then march to the station where a train would take them to Liverpool.

Near ten o'clock that evening, the remnant of the Royal Scots again marched through the Carlisle streets, smarter this time in new issued uniforms. Many more people came out on the streets and many more cheered, though some also wept to think that these survivors of a most horrendous tragedy were about to face a new ordeal, a new enemy in a distant land.

His reports and telegrams finished, Colonel Peebles joined them at the station. A grim and silent embarkation followed - so different from the one at Larbert, only that

morning but already seeming another world away. The
gathering midsummer darkness depressed the mood even
further and throughout the short night as the train rattled
towards Liverpool the men clung to the sides of the
carriage or to each other for fear of another catastrophe.

Nor could they sleep despite, as it happened, being
put into a train consisting entirely of first class carriages.
Indeed some of the survivors were to say that one lasting
legacy of the Quintinshill accident was that they had never
again been able to sleep in a train.

Eventually, sometime in the early morning, by which
time some of the men had been without sleep for two days
and two nights, they reached Liverpool.

Here they were put to sorting salvaged equipment and
later to carrying ammunition on board their troop ship, the
mail steamer *'Empress of Britain.'* Finally they embarked
the next day and joined their comrades from B and C
companies of the battalion, who were already aboard.

But as now they waited for the final preparations for
departure, and the tide to turn, word came that the men,
although not their officers, were relieved of their duty and
that they should return to their homes until further notice.
One of the uninjured officers, Lieutenant Riddell, went
with them.

What caused this change of plan is not recorded.
Perhaps one of Colonel Peebles' telegrams had struck a
chord - or maybe Sir James Spencer Ewart who
remembered the Royal Scots drawn up for their medical

parade at Carlisle Castle had over ruled the initial decision to send them on.

Whatever the reason, it wasn't long before the soldiers were marching again though the Liverpool streets towards the station. They had arrived in the early morning, when few people had been about, but they left in the middle of the day and so sorry a state did they present that those who saw them mistook them for prisoners of war and jeered at them while street children threw stones.

At least the journey home was swift. So swift that Albert Munro, a soldier from Bo'ness, who had managed to post a note to his parents from Liverpool saying that he was on his way home, found himself in Edinburgh before the post.

TWENTY-FIVE

All through the day hospital trains continued to bring the injured into Carlisle. Many more arrived in cars. Their reception proved problematic. The Cumberland Infirmary, the main hospital, had taken in a new batch of casualties from Flanders only last week and there had been so many of these that the Infirmary had had to despatch the less seriously wounded to be treated in auxiliary hospitals.

Mrs Parker, matron at the Cumberland Infirmary, had been on her early morning rounds when first she heard the news of the Quintinshill accident and though her information was limited she quickly despatched two nurses, the hospital porter and a quantity of bandages and dressings to the medical train that left Carlisle at 8.30. Back in her office, she took a constant stream of telephone enquiries: how many beds did she have? What operations could the Infirmary perform? Was she expecting any other patients? Above all what space could she make available?

Mrs Parker was a resourceful woman. When she began her round that morning, she knew she had four beds vacant in her Infirmary, but by 9.20 she had managed to increase this to thirty. The Flanders' wounded gave up their beds and lay on rugs and blankets in the corridors.

The first Quintinshill casualties arrived by car and after treatment they were put into the vacated beds. For the most part these were those who had been rescued early and who had not been critically injured. Mrs Parker had been arranging a meal for them when the medical train arrived back in Carlisle bring fifty emergency cases demanding immediate attention.

So these less critically injured soldiers, grateful at having found a hospital bed, now found themselves being turned out in their turn to make way for this new influx of patients.

Thereafter she diverted all the less seriously injured cases to auxiliary hospitals in the district and to the sick bay at Carlisle Castle; walking wounded she sent to hotels - only the most serious cases did she accept for the Infirmary.

Even so injured soldiers continued to pour in. They were carried into a large sitting room used by nurses and laid out on mattresses on the floor. By nightfall the number of beds that Mrs Parker had made available for the victims of Quintinshill had risen from four to seventy. She and her staff worked non-stop the whole of Saturday and up until three o'clock on Sunday morning by which time thirty-five emergency operations had been performed. It was a trying time, she said later with characteristic understatement. Apart from her normal and limited staff, she had only two extra nurses to assist who had happened to be on holiday in Carlisle and had offered their services immediately when news of the disaster reached them.

Some of the injured died on their way to Carlisle and many others were to die later, despite superhuman efforts on the part of doctors to save them. Still, sixty-two out of the seventy acute emergency cases for whom Matron Parker had found space were still alive the following Wednesday.

Carlisle threw itself into the work of assisting the injured. Motorists volunteered their cars to bring the injured to hospital. James Morton, who had been travelling from Derbyshire to Glasgow, broke his journey and made five return trips to Quintinshill returning each time with more injured soldiers.

Private citizens volunteered to help tend the wounded and provide information for relatives. The Carlisle Citizen's League became the central register for information about those killed, missing or injured in the accident. They took over catering operations and collected rugs, blankets, socks, shirts and towels from the public to send to the Infirmary.

The injured showed scant regard for themselves. A young Royal Scot, a private whose leg had been amputated and whose face and hands had been scorched by the fire, told a reporter that 'we could not have had a finer day for the accident' which, he continued, 'if it had had to happen at all could not have happened in a finer place.'

He was referring perhaps to the generosity of the people of Carlisle to whom all the injured were most grateful. One senior NCO told reporters that he would like to put his name to a document to thank local people who had come out and done so much to help. Had the calamity been their own Carlisle could hardly have done more or shown more sympathy with the influx of anxious wives and mothers who now descended on Carlisle searching for their soldier sons and husbands.

On the Sunday a detachment of less seriously injured soldiers posed for photographers on Carlisle Station, before being sent down to Preston for further treatment. Some carried sticks and leaned on the arms of friends; all were bandaged heavily but considered themselves lucky to be alive. Meanwhile the staff in the hospitals prepared those left behind for a flush of visitors.

Sir Charles Bine-Renshaw, Chairman of the Caledonian came in the company of other Caledonian officials, touring the hospitals and making a small cash donation towards their expenses.

At the Carlisle telegraph office extra clerks drafted in from Glasgow, Preston and Leeds, received anxious inquiring telegrams and tapped out replies of regret. The Citizens League provided what information they could but most of it was scant. In some cases soldiers had disappeared without trace, their bodies and even their identity tags having been consumed in the fire, mostly the picture was one of general confusion. With the injured sent to multiple hospitals and bodies sent to this mortuary or that, it was hard for anyone to know who was where. In consequence staff at the League's offices had a most trying time dealing with the constant stream of relatives who came looking for their loved ones on Sunday, Monday and Tuesday.

TWENTY-SIX

On the Saturday evening King George V sent a telegram to the Caledonian general manager, Donald Mathieson, expressing sympathy and asking for news of the injured. It read: *"The King is shocked to hear of the terrible railway disaster near Carlisle which has cost the country many valuable lives. His Majesty deeply sympathises with those who have lost relatives and friends, and trusts that you can send a satisfactory report about the injured."*

The King sent the telegram to Matheson's Glasgow office but he himself was already in Carlisle where eventually the King's wire caught up with him. In some haste, Matheson scribbled out an ample and unrevised reply for the clerks to tap out down the line to London. *"In reply to your telegram transmitted to me here, I beg to state with great regret for the information of his Majesty the King that as a result of collision near Gretna of south-going military troop train with local train the wreckage of which was immediately run into by express train from Euston at 6.50 this morning, about 115 passengers were killed and about 150 injured all with the exception of about six being soldiers, that is about 109 soldiers were killed of whom about 6 were officers. The injured soldiers, about 150 in number, were quickly taken to hospitals and hotels in Carlisle where they were visited this evening by Sir Charles Renshaw, Chairman of the Caledonian Railway, and me, and were found being carefully looked after by numerous doctors and nurses. All injured with a few exceptions doing well. We gratefully beg to acknowledge His Majesty's message of sympathy, which will be made known."*

Rather more concisely Field Marshall Earl Kitchener, then Secretary of State for War, wired to Sir James Spencer Ewart: "I am very grieved to learn of the terrible railway accident and the heavy loss of life. Please convey to the bereaved an expression of my deep sympathy and to the injured my sincere wishes for their recovery."

It was an age of telegrams and now Donald Matheson received a second from Buckingham Palace, this time from the Queen: *"The Queen desires to express her heartfelt sympathy with the relatives of those who have lost their lives through the railway disaster, and will be glad to send hospital comforts for the use of the injured if you will kindly inform Her Majesty what is most urgently needed."*

After quickly consulting Mrs Donald, the commandant of the nearest auxiliary hospital at Chadwick, Matheson wired to Buckingham Palace. *"Regarding the railway accident near Gretna, we beg to thank her Majesty for the gracious expression of sympathy and kind thoughtful offer to send hospital comforts for the injured, in which latter connection, inquiry reveals that fruit, chocolate and cigarettes would be acceptable. There are about two hundred injured soldiers in the Carlisle hospitals and if Her Majesty's gifts were to be addressed to the District Superintendent, Caledonian Railway,*

Carlisle, we would ensure their careful distribution amongst the several hospitals and be most grateful."

Official telegrams expressing similar sentiments and making anxious enquiries poured into the city. The Lord Provost of Glasgow wired to Lord Roseberry, Colonel in Chief of the Royal Scots expressing his *'profound horror at the appalling calamity'* and all over the country, but particularly in Glasgow and Edinburgh, committees passed formal resolutions expressing their deep grief at the terrible calamity and at the loss of so many lives.

Public figures speaking to this or that association praised the valour of the soldiers and attempted the impossible task of arguing that their short lives had not been wasted. In his presidential address to the Royal Society for the Prevention of Cruelty to Animals, the Marquis of Aberdeen said he felt the soldiers who had been killed had died just as brave a death as if they had actually been fighting at the front. He was certain, he avowed, that the thoughts of the soldiers were centred on one object alone, namely upholding the honour of their country.

And to the hospitals now came not only the Queen's gifts - which arrived on the Wednesday following the accident which was, coincidentally, her birthday - but gifts from individuals and institutions moved by the tragedy. Cadbury's for instance sent a large quantity of chocolate; Nicholson and Cartner sent picture postcards for the soldiers to write home on.

Everyone in Carlisle, it seemed, had wanted to send something, which, when it arrived, the hospitals duly recorded. Among the gifts were: butter, eggs, milk, fish, ham, bacon, lard, sausages, calves foot jelly, rabbits, soup, oatmeal, barley, sugar, salt, flour, bread, cakes, scones, teacakes, shortbread, rock, jam, rhubarb, asparagus, peas, tomatoes, potatoes, lettuce, apples, oranges, bananas, bottled fruit, washing soda, bedroom slippers, notepaper, towels, pillows, cigarettes, tobacco, roses and flowers. The generosity of Carlisle seemed to know no bounds.

TWENTY-SEVEN

As they lay in their hospital beds, recovering from their injuries, the Royal Scots perused the newspapers. On the Monday of that first hospital week - 24th May - they would have read that Italy had joined the Allies by declaring war on Austria, King Victor Emmanuel issuing a Royal Decree ordering the general mobilisation of the Italian army and navy. Two days later they would probably have picked up the Prime Minister's statement that he had completed his cabinet reconstruction with Lloyd George taking over responsibility for ending the shortage of shells and providing the ample supply of the munitions sorely needed by British armies in the field.

There was plenty of war news from France, too. But the Royal Scots would naturally have been more interested in the accounts from Gallipoli, whither, but for the accident, they would already have been on their way. *The Scotsman* carried a typical account prefaced by a customary three-decked headline:

NARRATIVES OF THE WOUNDED
TERRIFIC FIRE DURING LANDING

AUSTRALIANS BAYONET FIGHT

"*Stirring narratives of the Dardanelles fighting have been released to the Press Association's correspondent by French and Australian soldiers who have returned wounded to Alexandria.*

"*A French officer who had been in the fighting at Kumkala said that he had been in the trenches in France but he had never experienced anything like the intensity of the fire that met his troops during the, and subsequent to, landing on the Dardanelles shore. It was a perfect rain of shrapnel, machine-gun and rifle fire and the casualties suffered were heavy but the men were undeterred and showed the greatest bravery. Another French officer who was with the British troops on the other side of the straits said that the Dublins and Munsters were caught on barbed wire entanglements while attempting to land and that they were exposed to a murderous fire. It is said that the Dublins and the Munsters lost many men while the Essex regiment and South Wales Borderers were reported to have suffered severely.*

"*When the wounded Australians at the Victoria College (Hospital) received news of the rejoicings in the Commonwealth and New Zealand over their bravery, they set up a cheer and shouted 'We are going to do better when we get back.' They all describe the fighting as 'a great game - the best game they ever had.'*

'*We made them run,' said one Australian. 'We wanted to let them know what Australian steel was like, and they ran* screeching and howling before us; but,' he ominously added, 'we ran better.' Two New Zealanders were seen chasing eleven Turks, and the latter, terror-stricken were screaming and wailing."

Another report bore the title: THE ONSLAUGHT AT SARIBAIR

"Australian troops began the onslaught at Saribair. Packed into pontoons they were towed at great speed by destroyers, which, when near the shore, cut the hawsers and the pontoons ran on to the shore by their own impetus. They were met by a stinging fire of shrapnel and also machine gun and rifle fire, and the troops jumping out of the boats, waded neck high in the water to the shore. It appears that they did not land in the spot designated for them, and although they met with no barbed wire entanglements, the land was difficult of approach, and in the words of one of the men, 'they were submitted to a hellish fire'.

"Some of the men were drowned in the landing by the sinking of the boats pierced by shrapnel, but it is stated that the number was few. Once on land the Australians did not wait and they took three ridges in succession in a headlong rush. 'We had a running bayonet fight for three miles,' said one man, 'and many of our fellows went down, but nothing could stop us and many German officers met their deserts. Our big Australian lads lifted the Turks on the end of their bayonets and tossed them right over their heads. Oh it was a great game. We had gone off without waiting for our supports, and when we

155

got to the third ridge, we dug ourselves in, but the Turks were in greatly superior numbers here and we were obliged to retreat to the first ridge. Then the New Zealanders came along and off we went again, ploughing a way through the Turks, digging ourselves in here and there and waiting for the next opportunity. The casualties among our officers were heavy. Many had been picked off by German snipers. Some of our men spotted one of these fellows and seven were told off to round him up. He was behind a small hillock and we could see his head bobbing up and down. That German met his death from seven bayonet thrusts.'

"'Our Red Cross men worked magnificently and fearlessly, carrying off the wounded amidst awful fire. They never seemed to consider the risk of getting shot. Every one of them deserved the Victoria Cross. We found things getting a bit hot for us again, and we suffered severely in our second rush with the New Zealanders, but the Indian soldiers came along, and we got to the third ridge again and established ourselves there. The Indians fought with great coolness and determination, and were quite undisturbed by the hail of shrapnel falling everywhere amongst them.'"

"At the moment of writing it is impossible to ascertain the number of casualties. The Australians are reported to have four thousand wounded and the English one thousand. It is generally thought that the number of casualties of the first three days fighting must have totalled eight or nine thousand. The fighting is described as the

worst that any troops have been asked to undertake during the present war, and the heroism of the troops will certainly compare with that which has so far been witnessed in France. The fighting of the Australians and the New Zealanders is beyond all praise."

These reports provided the injured Royal Scots with some indication of what lay ahead for their friends and colleagues in 'B' and 'C' companies. They might also have considered that being injured and hospitalised in Carlisle might well be preferable to lying in the hot dry dust of a field station at Saribair.

TWENTY-EIGHT

Shortly after the accident the first rumours started to spread in Edinburgh and Glasgow and when the London express failed to arrive at Glasgow's Central station at eight o'clock, the friends and relatives waiting on the platform began thinking the worst. No-one seemed to know anything; at first it was given out that the express would be delayed by two or three hours. Then word arrived that a troop train had been involved in a collision but nobody could say from where this information had come. Railway staff remained tight-lipped and there were no official announcements.

The secrecy surrounding troop movements in wartime made matters worse. It was an offence to publish information about troop trains, for instance, without authorisation, so the Caledonian Railway felt that it could not say anything before such authorisation came through. As a result anxiety built on anxiety, rumour on rumour.

First people said that the ill-fated regiment had been the Cameronians; and then, no, that it had been the Royal Scots Fusiliers - a Glasgow regiment. Only much later in the day came the accurate information that the Leith Royal Scots had been involved.

The anxious crowds at the Central station grew in number as the long day wore on but when the first passengers from the doomed express did finally arrive in Glasgow, it wasn't at the Central station. The uninjured passengers had been directed to walk over the fields to Gretna Green, there to catch a Glasgow and South Western Railway train, which arrived at the St Enoch station about half past one.

A few newspaper reporters had had the perspicacity to realise that as the Caledonian mainline was almost certainly blocked, it would be sensible to keep an eye on St Enoch and this foresight proved lucky. From a small, bruised and worn group of travellers struggling along the platform reporters were able to glean the first eye-witness accounts of the tragedy and these figured prominently in the Monday editions of the Scottish press.

The first Caledonian train to arrive into the Central Station did not do so for another two hours, though this carried a larger number of survivors, including Mr and Mrs Terryer. The greater part, however, comprised soldiers and naval men who had been travelling in the express. Most bore signs of minor injuries.

Mrs Terryer required assistance in getting down from the train; her head was bandaged and she complained bitterly about the length of the journey from Quintinshill for this relief train had for some reason stopped at every little station and halt on the way taking almost four hours for a journey that would have taken an hour and a half by express.

Then, she said, there had been no refreshments! She'd only eaten a couple of scones, purchased from the buffet at Lockerbie at an exorbitant price. And even here they had run out of tea and she had had to make do with lemonade at 4 pence per bottle - a price that she considered even more extortionate than that of the overpriced scones. Against such indignities the wreck of her train seemed, apparently, a trivial hazard. But despite her bandaged head she had been much luckier than some.

Most of the men, the sailors and soldiers had assisted with the rescue effort and their uniforms were torn, scorched and blackened by the fire. An artillery officer, hatless and wearing only one boot, limped down the platform to where his relatives waited patiently for him. With his tunic torn and his face caked with blood from an injury to his forehead he later told reporters about the tragedy.

He had been asleep, he said, and, like others, had been pinned under the seat as the compartment had collapsed. Somehow he had managed to scramble out and to get five or six others clear as well. His name they noted as Lieutenant Lang, on his way home from special training at the range at Shoeburyness in Essex and with him travelled his friend 2nd Lieutenant Fairlie, whose uniform, the reporters noted, was also splattered with blood.

In a reversal of the usual roles, three young children now ran down the platform from the train and towards their father, an Able Seaman with HMS Mars on his cap band. Their mother, Mrs Gertrude Morby, followed with a baby in her arms. The family had been dozing on the express when suddenly all four had been pitched to the floor in a confused heap by the collision. A loud explosion followed, she said, which frightened her very much until a railwayman tried to reassure her by saying that it was only an escape of gas. It wasn't, she admitted afterwards, much reassurance, given that at that point they had yet to extricate themselves from the wreckage. But here they were now, safe and sound, and Able Seaman Morby from HMS Mars greeted each of them with a hug and a kiss.

These children were lucky. Another four children weren't. Their charred bodies, found in the wreck, were never identified and no-one came forward to claim them. They were buried later in the Glasgow necropolis.

Throughout that Saturday afternoon and into the early evening each train that came into the Central station from the south brought a few more survivors. The Caledonian authorities converted the station Waiting Room into a first aid post so that those arriving could be seen immediately by a doctor before being despatched to hospitals in the city. But of course many on the platform were disappointed when the faces of the loved ones they were expecting didn't dismount from the train. Many wept and for one man the shock was altogether too great for he collapsed and had to be carried out by staff to his car.

Charles Leggatt, the troop train guard, arrived back in Glasgow at 7.30 on the Saturday evening, his head heavily bandaged and his uniform spattered with blood. He had sustained a gash to his left cheek and eyebrow when the collision had knocked him off his feet and now he recalled for the benefit of reporters that he had happened to look out of his van at the moment of the collision and actually remembered seeing the troop train engine, three hundred yards ahead, rearing up immediately after the impact. Had he had the presence of mind to prepare himself for the shock, gradually transmitted through the long train, he would have had seconds in which to brace himself, but no doubt the image of the engine rearing up like a frightened horse transfixed him and he was sent sprawling when the shock arrived.

Meanwhile, over in Edinburgh, a hospital train drew into the Waverley station, bringing home 68 of the less seriously injured of the troop train soldiers. A large crowd had gathered on the station concourse behind barriers erected to keep them at bay and allow the Red Cross to help the soldiers, some of whom were stretcher cases off the train.

William Whitelaw, Chairman of the North British Railway, one of the Caledonian's competitors, waited on the platform to greet them with the battalion's former Colonel, Sir John Clark. He had come to see his nephew Lieutenant T.G.Clark, whose right hip had been painfully dislocated in the collision. Besides the lieutenant, the Red Cross had to take care of five other stretcher cases. The remainder of the soldiers had injuries to their heads or hands, but otherwise were able to walk to the ambulances booked to take them to the military infirmary in Craigleith. All the soldiers seemed in good spirits.

A second hospital train with 100 more Royal Scots, this time all stretcher cases, drew into Glasgow later in the evening. Among these some members of the crowd found a relative or loved one, but most did not and the crowd in and around the station did not abate much as the fine evening wore on. In the absence of hard news as to what had happened rumours of bombs, sabotage and German plots circulated freely among the crowds. Finally, towards midnight, a small train steamed in to the Glasgow Central's platform 12. It carried Sir Charles Bine-Renshaw, the Caledonian Chairman, Donald Matheson and the other Caledonian officials who had gone to Quintinshill and Carlisle on news of the accident.

Sir Charles appeared exhausted, but he read to the reporters waiting hungrily for news a short statement he had prepared on the train. He did not say much, partly, because at that point there still was little to say. The facts such as were known at the time seemed almost mundane: a troop train had collided with a stationery local train and a London express had run into the wreckage.

So Sir Charles emphasised instead the Company's extreme distress at the accident and the attendant loss of life. He supposed that the accident at Quintinshill would turn out to be the worst ever to occur upon a British railway. And in this he was right.

The reporters pressed him on the cause - but he could give them no information. With all the safety systems

164

designed to prevent collisions between trains it must have been inexplicable that such an accident could have occurred in the manner that it did. But he had no more information to give and after a few minutes, and with promises of a full statement at a later date, the reporters let him slip away from the dark station and into the night.

TWENTY-NINE

From Edinburgh and Glasgow, news of the disaster filtered rapidly out to Leith and the coastal villages from Bo'ness to Musselburgh. It didn't take long before the population of these stricken towns and villages began to realise the extent of the tragedy that had befallen their soldier sons.

As Saturday wore on and evening approached, the trickle of callers at the Royal Scots Drill Hall in Dalmeny Street, Leith, grew until it became a flood, blocking the road outside the building and surging angrily against the doors and windows. Anxious upturned faces, white against the dusk, demanded to know what had happened: had their been sabotage? a bomb? a conspiracy? How could soldiers go missing on their own homeland?

But the officers inside the Drill Hall knew little more than the crowd themselves and in some respects knew less. They knew that certain companies of the battalion had not been involved as there had been two trains and only one of these had crashed. But they had not been told (why would they be?) which companies had been on which train, and indeed which train, the first or the second, had been involved in the collision.   Nevertheless, unconfirmed word had come through that 'A' Company had been in the foremost part of the train and it was supposed therefore that 'A' company must have suffered more severely, if indeed 'A' company had been in the train that had crashed.

This long lack of information soon began telling on the nerves of the anxious relatives who became increasingly distressed and frenetic in their demands. Some broke down and sobbed uncontrollably. Others, bent by an urge to do something to obtain further news, hurried round to the Post Office and to the Leith premises of *The Scotsman* newspaper which that Saturday evening printed an extra late edition of its *Evening Despatch*.

But of course no reliable information was to be found in these places either and for the second or third time they hastened back to the Drill Hall in Dalmeny Street, where the telephone rang without intermission and where the two officers in charge - Major Smith and Major Muirhead - tried their best to give reassurance.   From time to time, again and again, the besieged officers shouted from the windows to the crowds outside - a message both of hope and terror that hung on the still evening air: *'there is no word yet.'*

The crush had hardly abated at midnight, so desperate were the crowd for information, and then finally at 2 am on the Sunday morning a list of those known to have escaped injury entirely was read out by Major Smith before being posted on the noticeboard outside the Drill Hall. This, no doubt, was the list produced at Gretna when the survivors had been summoned to muster. How and why it took ten hours to reach the battalion's Headquarters is unfathomable.

Some determined relatives remained all through the night but most now abandoned the quest for information and went home for a few hours rest. Next morning they returned and the crowd outside the Drill Hall swelled again, all clamouring to know how a railway accident in Scotland could have claimed over four hundred casualties.

Finally at eight o'clock on the Sunday morning came the official announcement that the members of 'B' and 'C' companies were safe. The train carrying these men south to Liverpool had been stopped at Lockerbie and then been diverted via Dumfries. But this just increased the pressure on those whose sons and brothers had been members of the other two companies.

From the twin villages of Musselburgh and Inveresk 120 young men had joined the battalion and been assigned either to 'A' or 'D' companies. The same list of survivors that had been posted outside the Drill Hall in Leith now appeared outside Musselburgh Police Station.

It soon became clear that Musselburgh would be counting a heavy toll. The telegraph office remained open all through that Sunday to receive messages that told of injury or death. The clerks handled 160 during the day. A few, sent briefly from Carlisle, or later Liverpool, confirmed that the sender was alive and well, but most contained tragedy. Like the one that arrived in Private William's home in Beech Lane, Musselburgh where his parents stared at the brief, but all too comprehensible words. 'The worst is feared,' they read.

James Stewart, one of Inveresk's Parish Councillors, opened a yellow envelope to read the better news that his son now lay in Carlisle Castle, with his foot amputated.

Mrs MacLaghlan received a yellow envelope from the messenger boy, too. She lived in the High Street, a widow since her husband and their two eldest sons had been killed in mining accidents. He had left her with three further sons. Of these one was already at the front in France and she feared for his safety. Her two remaining boys had both joined the Royal Scots and now this scrap of paper told her that, regretfully, William had been killed and of her remaining son, Tam, no trace could be found.

That Sunday morning the churches in and around Leith were even fuller than usual. Scarcely anyone among the large congregations was not related to, or had not known, at least one of those on the troop train. Preaching his sermon in South Leith Parish Church, the Reverend William Swan, one of the battalion chaplains, referred to the immunity from accident that had attended the transfer of hundreds of thousands of troops to France and elsewhere. To Leith, he said, belonged the sad distinction of being the first town to suffer in the person of its local regiment. 'We knew when our brave lads volunteered for the front,' he said, 'that suffering and death were inevitable.......There would have been a kind of glory if they had died on the battlefield, but they died without knowing the foe and that had added sorrow to sorrow.'

THIRTY

Information flowed steadily to the Drill Hall in Dalmeny Street throughout that Sunday. Major Smith and Major Muirhead now began to be in a position to say who had been injured, and how, and whither they had been taken. They posted new lists on the noticeboard outside. Yet for every man listed as injured another was listed as missing which the crowd found difficult to understand and the officers themselves were at a loss to explain.

How could men go missing during a railway accident in Scotland, the crowd wanted to know? All they could concluded was that they must be dealing with imbeciles and incompetents. Indeed, with no knowledge of the conflagration at Quintinshill, Majors Smith and Muirhead must also have found the number of missing hard to comprehend.

It was with some relief therefore that towards midday on Sunday they learned that a large number of unidentified dead soldiers had been taken to Carlisle and that a special train had been arranged, departing from the Waverley station at 4.30, to carry friends and relatives of the injured to that city. The train would leave Carlisle to return to Edinburgh six hours later at 10.30.

A great crowd, far greater than expected, gathered on the station platform. It seemed as though half the population of Leith wanted passage to Carlisle. Major Smith called them to order: the purpose of the train, he bellowed, was to take to Carlisle the relatives of those men known to be lying injured there, to expedite identification and to give relatives an early chance to communicate with the injured. He strongly advised that those who had no word of their menfolk not to travel as he had now heard that the bodies of the dead soldiers would be brought back to Leith later that evening.

Following this news a great part of the crowd stepped back, but 160 determined souls pressed on and received their return tickets to Carlisle, paid for by the War Office.

Major Smith travelled with them and so too did the Reverend Swan from the parish church in South Leith who had been deeply affected by the tragedy and was later to play a prominent part in its aftermath. Anxiety among the relatives mounted as they crossed the Border and a few minutes later approached the dark, cavernous vault that was Carlisle Citadel Station.

The railway authorities had sensed the mood of grief, too, for they excluded the public from the arrival platform. Only two officers from the military barracks at Carlisle Castle waited to meet them. Thanks to Colour Sergeant Creed, who had charge of the orderly room at the Castle and who had worked a spell of nearly twenty hours of continuous duty, the casualty lists had been updated and it was from these lists that Major Smith now read.

According to the list the death roll up to that Sunday night stood at 161 of whom 95 were unidentified or missing. The bodies of 66 Royal Scots had been identified including 3 officers. The total of injured soldiers in beds in or around Carlisle stood at 194.

As he read out each name, Smith asked any friend or relative to step forward so that they might be directed to the appropriate hospital or mortuary.

This all took some time but gradually the numbers on the platform dwindled as they left, singly or in small groups, to find the person whom they had come to seek. Among the remainder some women wept bitterly while others hung upon every phrase, praying under their breaths. Tearful sighs of thanksgiving followed the announcement of a son, brother, sweetheart found alive; soft groans from heads shaken in disbelief attended the adumbration of the dead.

Yet there were still a core left who heard no familiar name and so were left in pitiful suspense, their journey apparently in vain. Like so many others they could not understand how soldiers could be posted as missing even before leaving their native Scotland.

As the minutes ticked away on the great station clock and the hour of 10.30 drew near when the return train was due to depart, many of the relatives could be seen sobbing openly on the platform. The Reverend Swan went among them, doing his best to offer comfort. One young woman, he remembered afterwards, had been shaking with grief, having discovered nothing about her loved one. Suddenly she became still for across the way a young officer, his head and face swathed in bandages, stumbled towards her.

'Poor soul! What a smash he's got,' the minister remembered her saying and in her compassion for this officer, she appeared to forget her own grief. Imploringly she beseeched him for news, but like others he could offer no clue to the fate of the one she had come to seek.

Also disappointed were the relatives who learned that their injured menfolk lay no longer in Carlisle but had been transferred to Preston, though they had been relived to learn that these soldiers had been some of the most lightly injured. So when a south-bound train steamed into the station the authorities decided to offer the chance to travel on to Preston an offer that most quickly took up.

Others decided to stay on in Carlisle and not return on the 10.30 train. These included Councillor Scott, whose Bandsman brother - John Scott - had initially been reported killed but was later discovered to be lying at Fusehill hospital with only slight injuries. Such errors in the reporting of casualties were widespread.

In the immediate aftermath of the accident injured soldiers were despatched or taken here there and everywhere. Despite the efforts of men like Sergeant Creed and the Carlisle Citizens Defence league, many of those reported missing were missing only in the sense that they had not yet been found, no one having yet discovered to which hspital they had been taken. But of course there were soldiers that truly were missing, who had been consumed totally by the flames, leaving no trace whatsoever, even a dog tag.

THIRTY-ONE

That Sunday night, in newsrooms across Britain, editors were setting up the multi-layered headlines of disaster. That in the *Cumberland News,* published in Carlisle, ran to eight decks.

GRETNA RAILWAY HORROR
Over 160 Persons Killed
A REGIMENT'S UNHAPPY FATE
Three Trains in Collision
THE WRECKAGE A BURNING FURNACE
Vivid Narratives Of Survivors
How Carlisle Nobly Met A Great Emergency
BRITAIN"S WORST RAILWAY DISASTER

In their reports the papers banged the drum of passion, heroism and duty. The holocaust of Quintinshill had been a battle, the work of rescue a call to arms. If the accident had been a tragedy then it had also been a glorious and inspiring example to other boys and young men of a noble struggle against adversity. Hyperbole and fine words resounded as though noble sentiments could somehow transform tragedy and horror into victory and honour and turn painful loss into heroic gain.

The many acts of stoicism and self-sacrifice during the rescue inspired the leader writers. Thus in *The Scotsman*'s view: *"the beacon pile of Quintinshill was, for the men of the regiment, the shining light of duty,"*

While the *Leith Burghs Pilot* wrote that *"these men have died and the wounded have suffered for their country as truly as any who have found their graves or who have bled in Flanders or in France. The nation feels for them the same sorrow, holds them in the same honour and must surely give them, or their dependants, the same recompense.*

The Times described the disaster as *'an unexpected sorrow'* and, making its own tribute to the men who had painfully died, wrote: *"the sad news is deepened by the fact that nearly all who died were in the prime of manhood. Upon most of the dead we can look with the tempered pride and grief whereupon we can look on their comrades slain in action."*

A leader praised the military prowess of the Scots, so long a spearhead of British armies, and a constant pool of manpower. It continued *"They were soldiers and they died as Scottish soldiers die.......whether they were maimed or whole, they showed the steady discipline and tranquil courage of their profession and of their race."*

But the paper recognised that the savagery of the current war would soon obliterate all traces of the accident from the public consciousness. *"At a time when every hamlet in the land is mourning its own dead, the Gretna disaster cannot occupy the public mind so completely or for so long as do lesser calamities in ordinary times. We are in a school of sorrow and we have learned the lesson of fellowship in affliction."*

At that time the war had run only nine months of its terrible four year course, but *The Times* was right: except in railway circles, Quintinshill soon became an all but forgotten disaster, a footnote in the history books.

The enormous demands of the press put a great strain on the telegraph department at the Carlisle Post Office which was already handling an extra 500 private messages about the disaster. Through the Post Office, reporters filed 22,000 words on the Saturday and 55,000 on the Sunday. Even on Monday and Tuesday the reporters managed to file 34,000 words.

As ever a conflict raged between reporters with a story to tell and officials who believed that as little as possible should be disclosed beyond the bare facts. Sometimes this conflict itself became news with the *Glasgow Daily Record and Mail* protesting petulantly that *"both railway officials and police appeared to regard it as most important that as little information as possible should reach the public through the press......The employment of the police was to all appearances confined to preventing pressmen in the legitimate pursuit of their profession from approaching even within seeing distance of the scene."*

And from the safe distance of Glasgow the paper tweaked the constabulary's tail: *"policemen.....stood at the gates of fields adjoining the railway or stared vacantly into space in some sheltered corner. Evidently the importance of being a member of the Constabulary weighed heavily on their imagination."*

That fine Whit Sunday a throng of motorcars, cyclists and pedestrians clogged the road between Gretna and Carlisle. Those without transport trudged the ten miles from the city to the site of the accident and then trudged ten miles back again. As they walked they speculated again on the possible causes of the disaster. An accident must be ruled out, they concluded. A German spy must have tampered with the signal wires. That a troop train had been most heavily affected was proof and if further proof were required, why, the King himself had travelled over this line that very same week. That surely confirmed the matter, though no-one appears to have asked how.

The Cumberland News, however, denounced all such tittle-tattle in strong terms. *'These rumours have no foundation'*, it wrote. But still they persisted and when the following Thursday an axle in the bogie of a third class coach on the afternoon Midland railway express collapsed and broke half a mile short of the Citadel station and derailed the four rear coaches leaving much damage to the line in their wake, the German spy theory was taken out once again and dusted down and put into circulation.

THIRTY-TWO

The living and the dead returned on the Sunday evening. Lieutanant Riddell, led home to Edinburgh the bedraggled band of 56 uninjured survivors who earlier had been taken off the *Empress of Britain*. Arriving at the Waverley station they were rapidly bundled into motor ambulances and taken to the Craigleith military hospital for observation. At about the same time 106 coffins arrived at the Drill Hall in Dalmeny Street, Leith.

The authorities had issued little information about these homecomings of the living and the dead, but possibly as a result of Major Smith's remarks to the relatives waiting to board the train earlier in the afternoon, sorrowful crowds began again to gather in the early evening along Leith Walk and in front of the Drill Hall. They gathered outside Leith station, too and bit by bit the little knots of folk grew and swelled until they became a continuous thronging tumult.

Not all the folk had a direct connection with the Royal Scots; many came out of respect and solidarity with the bereaved, and stood sombrely, tears lining many faces.

An uncanny quiet lay over the town that continued until a Salvation Army band appeared at the foot of Leith Walk playing the Dead March from *Saul*. The sound of their brass instruments carried widely on the still summer evening air and people confessed that the sound of this music alone brought many of them to open tears.

At intervals between eight and nine o'clock contingents of soldiers arrived and stepped out into position along the route from the station to the Drill Hall, until they had lined the roadway. With this immaculate line of soldiery, their brass and leather gleaming in the dying evening night, the hushed expectancy of the crowds might have heralded victors coming home from some successful conquest rather than soldiers killed in a tragic accident upon the railway. Only the occasional jangling clatter of hooves and harness on the cobbles as a horse grew restless, or the random cry of a young child, broke the stillness.

Shortly before nine o'clock, the police suspended all ordinary traffic and a succession of funeral vans and motor ambulances left the Drill Hall led by a motor car in which travelled General Sir Spencer Ewart and other officers of the Scottish Command. Several doctors and a squad of ambulance men followed in a vehicle bearing a large red cross. The convoy passed along Leith walk and turned towards the station. By this time the crowds had swelled still further. Estimates put the size at 20,000 - perhaps the largest crowd ever to have been seen in Leith.

The funeral train arrived a few minutes later and the crowds in front of the station watched reverently as the soldiers began the slow transfer of the plain black coffins into the waiting vans. The work took a full half hour and then at twenty-five minutes to ten an officer's order brought the troops outside the station to attention and the cry of 'reverse arms' echoed back and forth as the sad procession left the station and turned south.

It moved at little more than walking pace and as it advanced each succeeding company of soldiers reversed arms in respect; even the quiet susurration of the crowd stilled. Then the ambulances returned to the station and the process continued for an hour during which time the crowd continued to wait and watch until the very last of the 106 coffins had been loaded and brought to the Drill Hall.

In these 106 plain black coffins lay 59 named remains of Royal Scots who had died on the troop train and, next to these, 47 bodies that no-one had been able to identify. The soldiers laid them out on trestles in a double horseshoe, each coffin draped with the union flag. Between the coffins they placed some pots of shrubs and palms. All the coffin lids were screwed tightly down.

The public now filed in and around the coffins. Those without a direct connection went upstairs and watched from the balcony. Relatives brought flowers, and if they could not find a loved one by whom to leave their flowers, they placed them on one of the unidentified coffins for, they said, after all someone's boy lay inside it.

To facilitate identification in the event of death every soldier wore a small numbered metal disc on a chain around his neck, usually referred to as a dog tag. In some cases this tag had been all that had been found beside, perhaps, some burnt remnants of what shortly before had been a living being. But where the fire had been fiercest, even the tags had burned away, or else melted and run into the ash so that there remained literally no trace. At best all that might have survived would be some battered trinket, the remains of a cigarette lighter, perhaps, with some engraving, or a button, and such poignant relics were laid on the otherwise unidentified coffins in the hope that someone would recognise them.

By such means did Mr Hendry, the miner from Niddrie, recognise his son whose identification disc had been burned away. For lying on the coffin lid he recognised the shamrock charm and the lucky farthing which the proud and anxious father had given to his son at Larbert. At the sight of these the miner broke down and wept and Major Smith had to assist him away.

Many others in that crowd also broke down at the sight of a trinket or a name on a coffin and had to be helped to move on. Among those assisting, the Reverend Robertson, one of the battalion's chaplains, tried his best to comfort the bereaved. Yet afterwards he also commented on the fortitude of the relatives: one woman who had lost her only son remarked through her tears that she was sorry she didn't have another to put in his place.

He thought this remark characteristic of many who had lost loved ones.

The body of Captain Mitchell, the timber merchant from Leith, who had been travelling in the first composite coach immediately behind the troop train engine, was never found, or if found could not be identified. Nevertheless, his brother officers sent a wreath to the Drill Hall. Many others, people and organisations, did so too, including the Town Council, and the Garrison Artillery Company from Leith Fort. The officers, NCOs and sergeants of the 7th Royal Scots second line battalion sent between them six wreaths so that soon the Drill Hall became a sea of floral tributes.

Just as the speed with which the Caledonian managed to clear the line of accident debris and to relay the tracks in a mere 36 hours - an achievement that would seems quite impossible today - so the funeral of the Royal Scots killed in the disaster was organised and carried out before the bodies had lain in Leith for more than 24 hours. By late on the Sunday evening the outline of the funeral had been decided upon. The Town Council had briefed the religious and cemetery authorities, consulted the military and arranged the form of the ceremony. The crowds waiting at the Drill Hall wanted only to know when. Monday, came the announcement, at five o'clock.

THIRTY-THREE

At a quarter past four the next afternoon, Monday, the Provost, Magistrates and Councillors of Leith, all wearing their formal robes of office, gathered in the Council Chamber to pass a formal resolution of condolence with the relatives of the dead.

When all were present, the window blinds were lowered as a mark of respect, shutting out the bright sunlight of summer. To the hushed assembly, now sitting in semi-darkness, Provost Malcolm Smith rose and formally moved the suspension of Standing Orders; he then addressed the Council.

'That so many young lives, the flower of this Community, who had by assiduous training for months - and some for years - prepared themselves for defending their country's interests on the battlefield, should thus suddenly and without warning be cut off, is sad and mysterious in the highest degree.'

Thus he began and he continued by listing the achievements of the battalion, speaking glowingly of their previous South African campaigns, and the warm spirit which had existed between the officers and men and between the battalion and the town. In certain places it seemed he had to struggle hard to contain his emotions as he spoke of the Town's hopes and of their expectations that this spirit of the Royal Scots would be matched by their prowess at the front; and he voiced the sorrow and sympathy of the community for the many bereaved homes in Leith that night.

When the Provost had finished, the formal resolution of condolence was read to the Council and to it they silently gave their assent. Staff then raised the blinds and the bright light of the warm and sunny afternoon contrasting so sharply with their sombre mood, flooded in upon the Councillors who now made their way to the Drill Hall; the public funeral of the identified Royal Scots was about to begin.

Earlier that afternoon, in the Drill hall, and under the watchful eyes of the bereaved, the two battalion chaplains, the Reverends Swan and Harvey, had commenced a short and simple funeral service for those soldiers whose identity remained unknown. In a secluded corner of Rosebank Cemetery, men of the Argyll and Sutherland Highlanders were already digging in the red clay the broad trench, eight feet deep and twenty yards long, that was to become the Royal Scots final resting place. Motor ambulances conveyed the black coffins to the Cemetery where these unidentified victims were laid shoulder to shoulder as they had once sought to fight.

Towards five o'clock, relatives of the identified dead were again admitted to the Drill Hall to inspect the remaining coffins for the last time and to lay fresh flowers. Their public funeral could now commence.

It was said that no funeral like this had ever before been seen in Leith or Edinburgh, or even in Scotland. The same vast crowds that had gathered the previous evening to witness the homecoming of the dead now turned out again and packed the pavements to pay their last respects. The great array of mourners reflected the numbers being interred, but there was something else too: for the funeral was to become a salute to all those who had fallen overseas in the first nine months of war and whose names appeared daily in the casualty columns of the press.

On that hot summer afternoon several thousand troops again lined both sides of the route from Dalmeny Street and along Leith Walk to the Cemetery gates. Most of the shops there had closed and put up their shutters and householders had drawn their blinds in respect. Incongruously, bunting put up to celebrate the Queen's coming birthday, fluttered from the lamp posts in the sunshine.

The funeral service itself began in the Drill Hall at five o'clock precisely. Again the battalion chaplains officiated, assisted by a Catholic priest, Father O'Rourke. Outside, two batteries of the Royal Field Artillery waited with their horses and artillery wagons and when the service was over, soldiers placed two coffins on each artillery wagon and draped both with the Union flag.

And then men from the King's Own Scottish Borderers began a slow march down Leith Walk, leading in silence the long cortege on its final journey to the cemetery at Rosebank. Behind the soldiers came the sharp clip of hooves on the cobbles and the jangle of harness as four immaculate horses rumbled each of the twenty-eight artillery wagons out of Dalmeny street.

Following the coffins came the pipe band of the 16th Royal Scots, magnificent in their parade dress, but their pipes remained unsounded as they slow-marched in deep silence over the first part of the route. Indeed an unlikely hush fell over the whole town as if it, too, were frozen in death. For a time the clatter of the artillery wagons seemed the only sound in a silent universe. But then the pipe band struck up, playing *'Flowers of the Forest'* the ancient Scottish lament for dead heroes, with majestic rolls on the kettle drums and a deep dull thud on the bass. The eyes of many in the crowd filled with tears.

Behind the band marched General Sir Spencer Ewart with his staff leading a distinguished array of public mourners including Provost Malcolm Smith and the magistrates and councillors of Leith. And behind them, stretching out into the distance, came the long column of private mourners, grief and sorrow etched in their faces.

As each artillery wagon passed, the soldiers lining the route came smartly to attention and reversed arms, their officers saluting the cortege as it rumbled slowly by. Outside the Cemetery gates waited the Salvation Army Band who again began to play the Dead March from *Saul*. The short period of calm that had hung over the cemetery since the last of the unidentified bodies had been interred was broken.

At the gates the cortege halted and a number of the dignitaries and private mourners now made their way through the gates where they stood in the sun in a great horseshoe around the great trench grave.   Inside this horseshoe, files of men from the King's Own Scottish Borderers took up positions flanking one side of the grave while the officiating clergy took the other. Wreaths and flowers of every description covered the great bank of red clay from the excavation of the grave.

For two hours they stood thus while soldiers bore the coffins from the artillery wagons to the graveside and the clergy pronounced words of committal and a blessing over each one. Lowered, then, into the grave, the coffins were laid in tiers of three with each tier covered with the union flag, while the pipe band played gently in the background and the evening breeze rustled the trees.

Eventually it was all over. The King's Own Scottish Borderers raised their rifles and three crashing volleys rang out over the grave and across the town, spreading the salute a great way over Edinburgh. And in the silence that followed the roar of the guns, and after the soldiers of the firing party had presented arms, a lone bugler sounded *The Last Post*.

Provost Malcolm Smith, on behalf of the Leith Town Council, then laid a large wreath at the graveside; others left flowers too and stood reverentially in the quiet moment. And then there was nothing left to do but to depart and leave the gravediggers to their work of filling in the grave. Only a solitary piper, Pipe Major Duguid of the 16th Royal Scots, remained by the tomb playing a last lament: *'Lochaber No More.'*

The crowds left the cemetery, but they didn't disperse quickly, staying on the streets until late in the evening. Even those folk who had no connection with the ill-fated battalion had nonetheless almost all got husbands, sons or brothers in the forces who might be killed just as swiftly and unpredictably, their bodies laid to rest perhaps in a shallow battlefield grave with no flowers or military salute and with only the acrid whiff of cordite to lament them. As one woman said, 'it could so easily have been my boy wha's in one of they coffins.' And so she came privately to say a prayer for the dead by the grave and another that her boy might come home from France alive.

THIRTY-FOUR

The following day, Tuesday 25 May 1915, Private Albert Munro, freshly discharged from Craigleith Infirmary, returned to his terraced home in Bo'ness. His parents and a crowd of relatives and well-wishers had come to meet him off the Edinburgh train and, while still on the platform with its limed curbs and pots of geraniums blooming in the May sunshine, had besieged him with questions about what had happened at Quintinshill.

A young woman seemed to recognise him and, stepping forward, she caught Munro's sleeve. Above the general clamour he caught the name Andrew Williamson, which she repeated over and over while looking imploringly at him. He heard her say that Thomas Barnett had been with him on the train and that Barnett had been Andrew Williamson's friend.

But all they had ever found of Thomas Barnett was a battered and burnt identification disc and no-one had been able to tell her anything about the other man. 'He was my brother,' she cried, wringing her hands. Munro could only shake his head.   His relatives pulled him away and eventually they just left her there, waiting on the station platform in the sunshine to meet the next train, just in case somebody had made a mistake and her brother might still return.

As it later transpired Andrew Williamson did not in fact die at Gretna. Nor was he injured, for he was one of those who survived the accident and had been taken to Liverpool to embark on to the *Empress of Britain* in Liverpool. But when the accident survivors were ordered off the ship and sent home he either chose not to hear the command or else perhaps was asleep. He therefore stayed on the ship and turned up in Gallipoli.

The same dramatic mixture of joy and sorrow, the same pity and pathos, was played out at each and every station along the Lothian coast. Of the 120 men from Musselburgh and Inveresk who had set off in such high spirits the previous Saturday morning, only twelve ragged and worn survivors now returned.   For every one family's joy, there were ten families plunged into grief or uncertainty.

The twelve survivors formed up and bravely marched through the town in salute to their fallen comrades. At the Town Cross, where they halted, they encountered a smart body of men, carrying musical instruments, and wearing new Royal Scots uniforms. They recognised them as the Musselburgh and Fisherrow Trades Band and the musicians said that when they had heard about the disaster they had decided to join the Royal Scots en bloc. Now at the foot of the Town Cross they played a hymn in memory of the Gretna men who had not returned.

They felt a little self-conscious, but also proud, for this was the first time that they had played together in uniform as soldiers ,but people appreciated their playing and said that with such spirit it would not be long before a phoenix would arise from the ashes of the tragedy.

The next day, Wednesday, 19 more victims were laid to rest in Rosebank cemetery with full military honours and amid scenes similar to those on the Monday. For the most part these were soldiers who had been taken to Carlisle in a critical condition and had since succumbed to their injuries. One Royal Scots sergeant and six private soldiers were also buried privately that day as was Captain Robert Scott Finlay who had been travelling on the express.

He was buried in Dumbarton, his coffin having been brought the seven miles from the family home at Boturich Castle on a gun carriage accompanied by his brother officers from the Argylls. Captain Finley had been a prize winning shot at Bisley and Darnley. The war had been particularly unkind to the Finlays: Robert's brother in law and two cousins had already been killed and his parents now wondered about the fate of their three other sons serving with the Colours.

Assistant Paymaster William Paton was buried, too, in Cathcart Cemetery in Glasgow and the wreaths and flowers were said to be so abundant that they filled the open carriage which followed the hearse.

Driver Frank Scott and Fireman James Hannah from the troop train were also buried that Wednesday in Carlisle's Stanwix Cemetery. Scott's coffin bore the simple inscription: *'Remains of Mr Frank Scott - found on the footplate.'* The pall bearers were fellow footplatemen. As the cortege passed the hospital at Chadwick the flag there was lowered to half mast. Those Royal Scots convalescing there, who were able to stand, lined up with Red Cross nurses at the entrance gates to show their respect and sympathy to the Engine Driver.

By the Thursday, with four full days gone, 'missing' had begun to mean 'lost.' Yet still the authorities could not produce a final death toll or say who exactly had been on the ill-fated trains. Large numbers of injured still lay in hospitals in Carlisle, Glasgow and Preston and the news now came that some of these were more seriously injured than had been first thought. But still the greatest number were those of whom the fire had left no trace. Twenty-five of these came from Musselburgh alone.

Sergeant Gibson, accountant; Corporal Somerville, brewer's clerk, Private Arthur Colville, gasman, Private Robert Borthwick, miner; Privates William Williamson, James Maxwell and John Vass, paper mill hands; Private Robert Hay, butcher, Private Robert Dugdale, bandsman - these were some of the Musselburgh men of whom no trace was ever found, who just disappeared in the inferno as though they and their belongings and their metal identity discs had never existed. John Vass's father and mother spent two whole days in Carlisle in a diligent search for their son, but they found nothing nor could anyone begin to give them any information and so they were forced to return to Musselburgh, imagining their son's terrible fate.

More days passed and some of the injured came home again from Carlisle among them Sergeant Fleeting who had so heroically held himself back while ushering his men to safety out of the burning train. Leith gradually picked itself up and went about its business again.

Some weeks later the Town Council called a public meeting to consider what steps might be taken to commemorate the men who had died at Gretna. Provost Smith thought that the grave of the Royal Scots should be enclosed with a railing and a tablet placed on the wall behind, indicating their names and how they had lost their lives. He had already, he said, been offered quite a sum of money for this work and perhaps a more general memorial might be considered in due course. The Reverend Swan reported that injured soldiers in Carlisle had also asked what was being done to provide a memorial to their companions who had died.

This seemed the general sentiment but the speakers at the public meeting also hoped that, following the disaster, that there would be no shortage of recruits to take their places. Meanwhile should there be a surplus of funds after the memorials had been paid for then perhaps it could be used to endow a bed in Leith hospital and the meeting passed a resolution to this effect. They also set up a committee to supervise the erection of the memorial and then made arrangements to hold a large number of recruiting meetings to find new volunteers to replace the men who had been lost.

THIRTY-FIVE

Lieutenant-Colonel Edward Druitt, Royal Engineers who held the position of His Majesty's Inspecting Officer of Railways, arrived in Carlisle on the Monday evening following the disaster. It fell to him to investigate the accident and to prepare a report for the Board of Trade. Immediately he let it be known that he intended to visit the scene at 9 am the next morning, which proceeding might avoid the necessity for 'any stoppage during the inquiry for the purpose of clearing up ambiguities respecting the positions of the trains and the formation of the line.'

Donald Matheson, the Caledonian's General Manager, and some of his staff accompanied Druitt and though by the Tuesday morning the tracks had been cleared and relaid, the gangers had had the foresight to leave behind markers indicating the positions of the locomotives and carriages as they found them. A few poignant reminders of the tragedy also remained: some charred wreckage, not yet collected, lay at the foot of the embankment while the blisters on the paintwork of the Quintinshill signal cabin attested to the fierceness of the inferno.

Druitt measured the positions of these markers from the centre of the cabin where Meakin and Tinsley had stood at the signal levers and block instrument on that fateful morning just three days before. Also measured were the positions of the signals, points and bridges and other features he thought might be of importance. Finally he inspected the signal cabin and when this had been done he returned to Carlisle.

Originally he had proposed to hold the inquiry in the Board Room at Carlisle Citadel station, but so great was the number of witnesses and their representatives and members of the press and public who wished to attend that the inquiry moved directly to the Cumberland County Hall.

Even this now began to look full for, in addition to press and public, twenty-five witnesses were due to face the Inspector, accompanied by seventeen representatives from the railway companies or trade unions. Some of the military also attended including an injured officer from the troop train. Yet although the great loss of life had given the tragedy a greater profile and therefore public interest than was usual in such inquiries, it was essentially a railway affair: why had the usual safety procedures failed on this occasion and what might be done in future to prevent a similar type of accident from occurring. Having returned from Gretna, Colonel Druitt opened the inquiry a little after ten o'clock.

Donald Matheson rose and asked the Inspector's permission to make a statement. He said how sorry they all were that the Colonel should have had to make this journey to conduct an inquiry into the sad and distressing circumstances of the accident. He expressed the Caledonian's regret and extended the Company's sympathy to all the relatives and friends of those injured or killed. The message was then endorsed by Mr Lightfoot, the solicitor instructed by the National Union of Railwaymen to look after the interests of employees. Responding Colonel Druitt added the condolences of the Board of Trade to those of the Caledonian and the NUR. The hearing of the evidence could now begin; the Quintinshill inquiry had started.

First called was Robert Kennedy, the signal man at Gretna Junction. Kennedy, a careful man of 38 years of age, said he had been a signalman for the last eleven years. Nothing unusual had occurred in his signalling that morning but he recounted his conversation with the Quintinshill signalman and described how Meakin had said that Tinsley would get a 'ride' that day. A murmur arose from the audience.

'Did the signalman always travel by that train?' asked the Inspector.

Kennedy paused wondering how he might give a truthful answer without possibly incriminating his colleague.

'I don't suppose I have *seen* him travelling more than three times all the time I have been at Gretna,' he replied. 'Have you noticed him pass your box in the mornings?'

'I have noticed him *walking* past.'

'What time in the morning?'

'I have seen him pass between 6 and 6.30. That was the usual time: sometimes five past, sometimes ten past and sometimes just about six o'clock.'

There was an air of finality to his answers and the Inspector did not press the point, but went on to ask about the times of the trains.

With the aid of an extract from his log Kennedy recalled the times at which he had signalled the *Parly* and the two London expresses to Quintinshill and said that Tinsley had offered him the troop train at 6.47, the same time that he had offered the second express to Quintinshill. He described how he had waited for the troop train for several minutes before ringing up Tinsley to inquire where it was. A ripple of excitement went through the audience as he described Tinsley's hysterical response. Kennedy told the Inspector that he had observed Quintinshill's 'Obstruction Danger' signal and had put all his signals to danger before wiring for assistance to the Stationmaster at Carlisle.

Druitt told him to stand down and called the signalman to the north of the Quintinshill box - Thomas Sawyers, from Kirkpatrick-Fleming.

Thomas Sawyers told the inquiry that he was 35 years of age and had been with the Company now for seven and a half years, the last three of these as a signalman. After consulting his log he told the Inspector that Quintinshill had offered the 5.50 express at 6.33 which he had accepted at the same time. The 'entering section' signal had come at

6.38 and the express had passed his box at 6.42. He had received the offer for the 6.5 express five minutes later, at 6.47, and he had accepted that train immediately, too. According to his log, he said, he had then received an 'entering section' signal for the 6.5 express at 6.53.

The Inspector glanced sharply at him for if this was true then it was remarkable. For the 6.5 express never reached the Quintinshill-Kirkpatrick section having come to grief just a few yards outside it. How then could the 'train entering section' signal have been sent?

'What was the next thing you received?'

'I received the 'obstruction danger' signal at 6.53. Directly *afterwards* I got the 'entering section' signal.'

'Which did you get first?' asked Druitt.

'I got the obstruction danger signal first. I got it before I got the 'entering section' signal.'

'Are you quite sure?' asked Druitt incredulously.

'Certain,' replied Thomas Sawyers emphatically.

Among those attending the inquiry a picture was already building up of chaos and confusion in which signals were sent to warn of the coming of trains that had already crashed.

With the aid of his log Thomas Sawyers went on to give the Inspector further details of the times of his signals. He had offered the train of empty coal wagons to Quintinshill at 6.17 and this had entered the section at 6.25. He said he had received the 'out of section' signal for this train at 6.34 but he had not received any 'blocking 'back' signal which would have prevented him from sending forward any further trains.

'Was the troop train going fast when it passed your box? asked the Inspector.

'Yes, it was running fast' came Sawyers' reply.

The signalman stood down and Druitt, having a moment earlier received a message, announced that he would now be adjourning the inquiry for a short while to enable him to attend at the City Police Office where the Carlisle Coroner was about to open the inquest into the deaths of those who had succumbed to their injuries in Carlisle's hospitals.

The interruption was brief enough. The opening being just formal and the inquest then adjourned. So Druitt was able to resume his own inquiry at 11.30, calling Driver Moss of the Carlisle goods train to give evidence. Moss said he had been a Caledonian driver for 25 years and on that particular morning had driven the scheduled 4.50 goods from Carlisle, although their departure had been delayed until 5.50. The train had been composed of 45 loaded wagons.

'Did you notice the up main line signals at all before the accident? asked the Inspector.

'No sir,' replied Moss. 'After the troop train passed, however, I looked at them and they were lying off.'

He told the Inspector that he had first noticed fire immediately after the second collision near the leading engine of the express which had reared up in the air.

'Everything was burning together, splinters from the

carriages I would say. The engine had covered itself with debris as it came through and this caught fire. there was also a separate fire amongst the carriages on the other side.' Moss said he didn't know the cause of that.

Driver Moss then described how he and fireman Watson had drawn the undamaged portion of the goods train clear of the accident. He also told how they had returned later with their engine to fight the fire. Asked how he thought the fire had started, Moss said he thought that burning cinders from the ashpans of the locomotives were to blame.

Interest then quickened again among press and public in the County Hall as the Inspector announced that he would call George Meakin, the Quintinshill night signalman, as his next witness.

THIRTY-SIX

According to a reporter from the *Cumberland News,* Meakin appeared worn and anxious, as well he might given that the fundamental cause of the accident was a grave signalling error. Nevertheless, he reasoned, the accident had not taken place on his watch. It wasn't he that had pulled the fatal signals.

Meakin told the inquiry that he was 31 years of age and had been with the Caledonian since leaving school at the age of 14. He had been a signalman for ten of these years, the last three at the Quintinshill box.

'On the morning of the 22nd, what time did you leave duty? the Inspector began.

'My mate relieved me at 6.32.'

'Why was he late - do you know?'

'I cannot say; sleeping in a little I expect, sir. We made it our duty to change between 6 and 6.30.'

The audience exchanged knowing looks as though signalmen could not be expected to get out of bed in the morning.

'How did he come that morning?' asked the Inspector.

'On the engine of the local train.' replied Meakin, and again a ripple of excitement ran through the audience. This was most irregular, as Druitt showed with his next question.

'Had you the authority of your inspector, or of anyone else, to change duty in this way?' he asked, somewhat rhetorically.

'No, sir,' replied Meakin.

It was clear that Meakin himself attached little significance to such an irregularity. Railwaymen often worked out such mutually beneficial arrangements.

'You did it by yourselves without authority?'

'Yes.'

Having established the point Druitt asked to see the Quintinshill train register book and spent a couple of minutes perusing the entries, then he handed it back to George Meakin.

'Now tell me from your book the times of the local train from Carlisle.'

'It was offered to me at 6.20 am and I accepted it at 6.20.'

'What time did it arrive?'

'6.30.'

'And then what did you do with it?'

'My mate came into the box off the engine of that train.'

'What did you do with the local train when it arrived?' persisted Druitt.

'I put it from the down on to the up line, through the crossover road,' answered Meakin, explaining to the Inspector that he did so because the down loop line - into which he otherwise would have put it - had been occupied by the Carlisle goods train. He went on to say he had received instructions not to send the coal empties train on to Carlisle but to hold it at Quintinshill.

'What did you do with it?' asked the Inspector referring to this coal empties train.

'I put it into the up loop.'

'What time did you put it inside the loop?'

'It arrived clear of the loop at 6.34.'

'Did you replace the loop signal?'

'Yes, the loop signal and points.'

'At 6.34?'

'Yes.'

The Inspector now inquired about the information that Meakin had given Tinsley when the latter arrived in the box at 6.32 and Meakin recounted the positions of the trains and the telephone call which told them that the troop train had passed Beattock at 6.17.

'Did you tell him about the local train being put through the crossover road to the up road?'

'Yes,' confirmed Meakin.

'And at that time there was a train in each of the loops and the slow passenger train had crossed over from the down line to the up line?'

'Yes,' repeated Meakin.

'And you made your mate acquainted with all that was done?'

'Yes, I left off work at 6.35 or 6.36.'

'What did you do than?'

'I sat down and read the paper in the cabin.'

'Did you talk to him?' asked the Inspector, referring to Tinsley.

'There were a few remarks passed.'

'Did you read the paper out to him?'

'No. I don't think I read the paper out; I passed two or three remarks.'

Druitt then turned his attention to the other men who had come into the signal box cabin that morning. Seated in the dark, high-backed chair at the front of the hall he listened carefully to Meakin's replies and made occasional notes. Meakin described how the brakesmen had come to the cabin and the length of time each had stayed. He told the Inspector how fireman Hutchinson from the local *Parly* train had come up to sign his name in the book and that he had stayed four or five minutes in the cabin. He said it was usual for the brakesmen to come when their trains were waiting. Druitt then asked whether Meakin had paid any attention to what Tinsley had been doing after the handover and Meakin replied that he had not.

'What was the first warning you had of anything being wrong?' asked the Inspector.

'When the troop train was coming past the box. I was just going home then.'

'What speed?' inquired Druitt laconically.

'I should say about 40 miles an hour.'

Meakin then described how he had run back into the signal box and had been asking about the express at the time of the second collision. He recalled how he had thrown the distant signal to danger and the Inspector noted this.

THIRTY-SEVEN

At this point in the enquiry George Meakin appeared fairly confident. After all the accident had occurred nearly twenty minutes after he had handed over responsibility for the box and more than fifty minutes after his shift was due to end. Had he not stayed behind to read the newspaper he might have been home by the time the crash occurred. And although he was now wishing fervently that he had hurried back to the Maxwell Arms on that fateful morning instead of snatching a few minutes relaxation after completing his work, he still felt he was on fairly safe ground. After all, he reasoned, he had always done his job to the best of his ability and no-one had ever complained of his work nor found anything untoward in the working of his box. Moreover, it was not he that had arrived late that day, nor pulled the fatal signals.

But as the Inspector's questions bore down upon him he began to feel less confident; beads of sweat broke out upon his brow. He wasn't used to such proceedings, nor had he often faced such a hostile atmosphere. His anxiety increased as the Inspector resumed.

'Before you handed over to your mate, what was the last signal on the block instrument?'

'Accepting the 5.50 from Carlisle.'

'What time?'

'6.33.'

'From Gretna Junction?' queried the Inspector.

'From Gretna Junction,' confirmed Meakin.

'You gave train out of section for the local train?'

'Yes.'

'After you put the empty coal train into the up loop did you give *'out of section'* for it'?

'No, sir,' replied Meakin with emphasis.

'Although you replaced the points and signals?' queried the Inspector. 'Why did you not complete the movement for that train?'

'My mate was standing working at the block at that time.'

There was no reason why this should not have been so, but the Inspector persisted with this line.

'You know that on the block instrument there is an indicator lock?'

'Yes, but I never released the indicator lock,' said Meakin deliberately.

'You cannot clear a section without deliberately plunging that lock.'

'I did not do it,' reaffirmed Meakin.

The Inspector switched tack. 'When you crossed the slow passenger train, did you give the 'blocking back' signal?' He reminded the inquiry that this signal of two

214

beats on the bell followed by a further four blocked the line to the rear of the signal box and prevented the signal box behind from offering any further trains forward until the block had been cleared. It also switched the block indicators to 'on' (for train *on* line).

Meakin replied that he had not given the 'blocking back' signal for the simple reason that the coal empties train was still on the line and had not yet been given 'out of section.' This signal would need to have been sent first, he explained. While the coal empties train was on the line, the block indicators were 'on' and the local train was therefore protected. He would have needed to clear the block first before he could have given the 'blocking back' signal. Meakin's explanation was quite defensible.

'Would you have given the 'blocking back' signal afterwards if you had been in charge?'

The answer was obvious. Meakin affirmed that he would have sent the signal just as soon as he had cleared the points and given the 'out of section' signal for the coal empties train. The reason that he had not done so was that by then Tinsley had taken over and was working at the block.

'Why did you not complete all thee operations? You ought to have completed them. You ought to have seen what he was about.'

To this barrage of questions Meakin could only repeat that as Tinsley had already started working at the block and that as the latter was a fully trained signalman, he had assumed that Tinsley would be giving the appropriate signals himself. It wasn't his job after all to supervise his mate. But he doubted that his answers were convincing members of the audience.

Meakin must have wondered whether perhaps he should have replaced the loop points and signals - his last action in the box. He could have left that task to Tinsley, but as the latter was at the block and occupied with writing up the 17 entries in the train register book, replacing the points and signals seemed no doubt like a kindness.

Druitt made a few notes and pressed on. 'Did you make use of the lever collars?'

Lever collars were additional safety devices consisting of iron rings which slipped over the handle of a signal and prevented the safety catch being released. Putting a collar on a signal would this prevent it being used until the collar had been lifted off. The collar would remind the signalman that there was some reason why the signal should not be pulled.

'No, it is very seldom that we use them,' answered Meakin, wincing at this admission, for a lever collar would have certainly prevented the accident in this case as the Inspector also made clear with the following remark.

'Had the lever collars been used in accordance with the company's instructions, they would have prevented the accident,' averred the Inspector.

It was becoming clear to Meakin that the ground he stood on was not nearly as stable as he had once thought. His defence depended entirely on his being able to show that he had handed over the box to Tinsley in a safe condition. He had no reply to make to the Inspector's statement about the collars which he knew was true.

'Why don't you carry out your instructions?' demanded the Inspector peremptorily. To which the hapless Meakin could only reply, 'we thought the blocking back signal would do.'

'But you never gave the blocking back signal,' retorted the Inspector. If Meakin replied his answer was inaudible.

THIRTY-EIGHT

The Inspector had made his point and though he asked a few more questions including how long it took Meakin to walk to work, he ascertained nothing further of substance. So he handed over the questioning to Mr Lightfoot, the solicitor who was there to defend the railwaymen's interests.

The mitigating circumstances that the solicitor established were however limited, though he did draw from Meakin, first the fact that that night had been a particularly busy one and, secondly, that, as the local train would have passed Tinsley, after he had stepped down from the engine as it had reversed through the crossover and on to the up line, it was indeed reasonable to infer that Tinsley knew just where the local train actually was.

The lever collars, Meakin suggested, were used principally to protect a train or vehicle left in the loops which were not a part of the block system. Meakin also said that it was usual for brakesmen to come to the signal box to make inquiry as to how long their train might be delayed, but that there was no nonsense going on.

When Mr Lightfoot had finished with Meakin and he had stood down, the Inspector called James Tinsley to the stand and the spectators watched with great interest as the little man prepared to give his evidence. It was clear from his demeanour that the shock and responsibility of the accident weighed heavily upon him. Both he and Meakin had been suspended from duty; this was perhaps natural before an inquiry, but Meakin - at least before his questioning by the Inspector - had been pretty much convinced that responsibility for the accident could not be attributed to him. Tinsley, on the other hand, seemed only too well aware that his actions had caused the appalling lost of life.

So he appeared distraught, as well he might, and his initial answers to the Inspector so lacked coherence that Mr Lightfoot asked the Inspector's permission to speak to James Tinsley in private. He may well have encouraged the signalman to tell the Inspector all he could and to be as open and honest as possible and if he did do this then he was successful for the signalman's answers became more audible and straightforward from this point.

Aged 32 he had been in the Caledonian's service, Tinsley said, for ten years and a signalman for eight, five and a half of which had been spent in the Quintinshill box. Druitt began, as with Meakin, by referring to the changeover of shift.

'On the morning of 22nd - what time did you come on duty?'

'6.33 answered Tinsley'

'What time did you sign in the train book as having come on?'

'I signed as having come on at 6 am.'

'Has it been a practice between you and your mate to come to some arrangement so as to avoid coming out too early in the morning?'

'Yes,' answered Tinsley, faintly. And then, perhaps remembering what Mr Lightfoot had told him, he went on to say that he nearly always came on duty about 6.30 and that he got a lift with the local train as often as he could. He described the arrangements for making entries on the telegraph forms and told the Inspector of the circumstances attending his arrival at Quintinshill that Saturday morning. He confirmed Meakin's account of how the latter had brought him up to date with the train movements expected at the box.

'What was the first block signal you performed?' asked the Inspector.

'The first signal was at 6.38. I accepted the 5.50 express on the down line at 6.38.'

'On the up road, what was the first signal you performed?'

'It was for the special troop train.'

'Had you anything to do with the coal train?' asked the Inspector.

'No!' insisted Tinsley. This remark directly contradicted Meakin's evidence. Meakin had said that Tinsley had gone directly to the block instrument on entering the cabin and had given the train out of section signal for the coal empties train at 6.34.

'When were you offered the troop train?' continued the Inspector. Tinsley consulted the train register book. 'I was offered the troop train at 6.43 and I accepted it.' I offered it to Gretna at 6.46 and received the line clear signal for it. I pulled off the signals for it.'

Here Tinsley paused and then as if trying to get something off his chest he said, quite deliberately, 'I quite forgot about the local train.'

This startling admission induced a ripple of shock and disbelief among the audience. But the fact was that safety systems were designed so that a railway might be run safely even by signalmen with deficient memories. Tinsley continued.

'When I got to the box, the block indicator for the up line was in its normal position and not showing 'red' which it would have shown if the block were not clear.'

'Someone must have put that (the blocking indicator) back after the (coal empties) train had entered the loop,' concluded the Inspector.

'Someone must' agreed Tinsley.

'Are you quite sure you didn't?' probed Druitt.

'Quite sure,' insisted the signalman.

There is no way of knowing which of the two signalmen were telling the truth here and indeed neither of them may have had a clear memory of that one small isolated event - clearing the block and sending the 'train out of section' signal in respect of the coal empties train.

At best it is hard to remember a small routine action performed so many thousands of times before when there is no particular reason to do so and especially when, as in this case, both signalmen's memories were swamped by the accident that followed twenty minutes after the signal.

Tinsley's defence would be that the safe running of trains should not, and did not, rely on human memory, fallible at the best of times. He argued that as the block was clear when he accepted the troop train, he could not be faulted if he had forgotten about the troop train; he should not be held to blame if others had not deployed the correct safety procedures.

THIRTY NINE

While there is no direct evidence that points to Tinsley as having given the fatal *'out of section'* signal that cleared the line, several indications suggest that it would have been surprising had Meakin done so.

First, had Meakin given that signal there would be no reason for him not to have then given the 'blocking back' signal immediately afterwards. It was later to emerge that he had performed this sequence of actions many times before and being a responsible signalman he would, almost certainly, have completed the signalling in respect of the local *Parly* train, including giving the 'blocking back' signal unless he were interrupted, as he said, by Tinsley taking over the duty from him.

Secondly, there were already 15 entries to be copied into the train register book from the loose telegraph form and Meakin would not have wanted to add to the list once his mate was in the box. This suggests that he would have avoided any block signalling after Tinsley had arrived. Last there is no reason in any case to suppose that Meakin should have wanted to go on signalling once his mate was in a position to take over. Replacing the loop points and signal was an automatic reaction to protect the line when the coal empties train had drawn into the loop and a preliminary to any signalling done on the block. Tinsley would in any case have been busy in writing up the 15 entries at this time (6.34). The evidence therefore seems to suggest that the fatal 'out of section' signal, which cleared the block, was given by Tinsley.

Neither shall we ever know the true frequency with which Tinsley travelled to work on the footplate of the local train, whether or not it was necessary to shunt it at Quintinshill. After the event it seems strange that in none of the subsequent inquiries into the accident was this point ever fully explored. It was commonly accepted both at Druitt's inquiry, and at the subsequent coroner's inquest and criminal trials that followed, that Tinsley happened to be riding on the engine of the local train because, that particular day, it was due to be shunted at Quintinshill.

But the *Parly* was not regularly shunted at Quintinshill; in the previous six months - say 156 journeys - it had been shunted at Quintinshill only 21 times. Now, if Tinsley were to reach the Quintinshill box on foot by 6.30 (let alone an earlier time) he would have had to have set out from his cottage at Gretna between five and ten past six, by which time he would not have known whether the local was to be shunted or not. Moreover, if he had waited at Gretna until the *Parly* arrived at 6.25 to inquire whether it was to be shunted and then had found that it wasn't and then had to walk, he would not have reached the Quintinshill box until about 6.50, which would have been dangerously late in view of the frequency with which the Quintinshill box was inspected. In any case why would Meakin consent to such a regular delay in his arrival?

It seems more probable therefore that Tinsley's regular practice was to travel by the local train whenever he was on the morning shift - which was one week in four. The driver could easily have slowed at the Quintinshill home signal to let him off and such practices, though contravening regulations, were not entirely unknown on the railway.

If this were in fact the case then Tinsley's lapse of memory becomes more explicable for it would have been routine for the *Parly* to have passed out of his mind as soon as he had dropped off from it. His first regular signal on the block would then have been a 'train out of section.' to Gretna. On this occasion, did he follow routine and being accustomed to giving such a signal, gave one automatically (although on this occasion on the other block instrument) as soon as he reached the box? Such is speculation but it would appear to accord with the facts. If Tinsley, when on morning shift (and this was the sixth day of the week) normally rode on the *Parly,* and simply dropped off when it slowed down, then in his mind the road would be clear. In these circumstances it is easy to see how the lapse of memory might possibly have occurred.

The Inspector did indeed question whether Tinsley had been able to see the engine of the local train which had been standing only thirty yards or so from the signal cabin when Tinsley had cleared the line for the troop train. The signalman had to confess that he wasn't normally in the habit of looking out at the line when he pulled off his signals. 'There wouldn't be time,' he said. Besides, he could see the semaphore arms quite clearly from the signal frame. The Inspector changed tack.

'What time were you offered the second express?'

'6.46, and I accepted it and offered it forward to Kirkpatrick.'

'What time did you get the 'enter section' signal?'

Tinsley consulted the train register book: '6.48.'

'When the collision with the troop train and the slow train occurred did you realise that the express was just approaching?'

'I knew that the express was at the back of it after it had happened. I could not say where,' replied Tinsley.

'Did you put your down signals to danger at once?'

'They were all put to danger as soon as the accident happened. I cannot mind now who put them at danger.' Tinsley sounded confused.

'Did you put them at danger?' persisted the Inspector.

'I cannot say,' said Tinsley unwilling to commit himself.

'Your mate was still in the box,' suggested Druitt.

'Yes.' Whether Tinsley was unwilling to give Meakin credit for returning to the box and putting the down signal to danger for him or whether his memory of events had been so swamped by the magnitude of the disaster is unclear.

The Inspector continued his questioning, now on the subject of the other men in the signal box. Here Tinsley confirmed the evidence given earlier by Meakin. he also said that he had given his pen to Hutchinson, the fireman from the local train, so that the latter could sign his name in the train register book.

'That ought to have reminded you that the train was on the road,' ventured the Inspector.

'Yes, it ought,' agreed the luckless signalman.

'What were you doing between the time of your arrival in the box and the accident?'

Tinsley thought for a minute. 'I said to my mate there would be another express to come and he said 'yes.' I rang up Number 3 cabin (Carlisle) and asked where the second express was. The boy said that it had passed him at 6.40. I went to the desk where the book was after taking my jacket off, and I looked through the book and the forms to see what trains were marked down.

Strangely the Inspector did not then ask about the number of entries or how long it had taken Tinsley to copy them into the book but went off on another line of questioning entirely.

'Are you accustomed to making use of the lever collar when a train is in the section?'

'Just to indicate when a train is in the loop.'

'Why did you not make use of it on this occasion?'

Tinsley did not answer this directly but implied that he thought that the local train would be protected by the 'blocking back' signal, which he assumed would have been made. He had not thought to give this 'blocking back' signal himself because by this time he had forgotten all about the local train being on the up line.

All seemed to hinge on the one ordinary, but in the end fatal, block telegraph signal giving 'train out of section' for the coal empties train and clearing the line. The Inspector returned to this now.

'Are you quite sure you did not give the 'out of section' signal for the empty coal train?'

'Quite sure - the first signal I gave was at 6.38,' replied Tinsley, sticking to his defence.

FORTY

Mr Lightfoot, the National Union of Railway's solicitor now took up the questioning and he led the signalman to state that there had been nothing amiss with his mental or physical state that morning. That avenue of mitigation being closed, he tried another.

'Would the fact that the empty train on the up loop line standing immediately in front, not prevent you from seeing the up line?

'A wee bit?' answered Tinsley, yet the reality was that from his position of vantage in the box a signalman could look down quite clearly across all four tracks should he choose to do so.

Lightfoot also led Tinsley to say that there had been no time between the two collisions to have taken any action which could have stopped the express. This was unfortunate, and also untrue, as from reconstructions carried out later, in which Guard Graham and the footplatemen, Benson and Grierson retraced the steps they had taken to warn the express, it was clear that there was anything between one and two minutes between the collisions. It is virtually certain that the express was well outside the down distant signal at the time of the first collision and had Tinsley reacted even half-promptly, the second, and in terms of loss of life, much more devastating collision, could have been prevented.

The Caledonian Superintendent of the line, Mr T.W.Pettigrew now challenged Tinsley about the indicator lock and the signalling for the coal empties train, but Tinsley was unshakeable and he repeated that the indicator was showing 'off' when he accepted the troop train. Pettigrew also pressed him about the signalling after the first collision, but Tinsley's memory continued to be hazy.

'I may have put the up line (signals to danger) but I am not sure about the down line signals,' was all he could offer.

Druitt seemed to be becoming a little irritated about this point; he recalled Meakin to the stand.

'Did you put the down line signal to danger before the second collision?' he asked Meakin directly.

'The down line distant,' replied Meakin, glad to have a chance to say something that might be construed in his favour. 'I do not believe I put the home signal (to danger) because the collision had occurred then. As soon as I turned round and asked my mate, I rushed to the signal and pushed it to danger. At that time the second collision happened. Perhaps I put the home signal to danger, but I cannot remember, I quite well remember putting the distant signal to danger.'

Both Druit and Pettigrew then asked Meakin further questions about the coal empties signalling and the

232

indicator lock but Meakin was 'quite certain' that he had not given the 'out of section' signal and repeated his evidence about Tinsley proceeding directly to the block on entering the cabin. The Inspector stood him down.

There was time before lunch to call just one more witness and the Inspector called Thomas Ingram, the brakesman of the goods train. He told the inquiry that he had been thirty years in the Company's service, a brakesman for the last eighteen. He said that he had gone to the signal box to see how the expresses were running and how long his train was to be kept in the down loop. He had heard the two signalmen talking about the running of the trains but he had not observed, he said, any signalling on the block instruments. He had left shortly afterwards and had been up in front of his train when the first collision had occurred. He noticed the fire, he said, 'practically at once,' after the second collision. Five wagons on his train were practically buried and the fire spread very rapidly, the barrels in the wagons burning easily, although he could not say what was in them. The Inspector was not learning anything new so he stood him down and adjourned the inquiry for lunch.

When it resumed Druitt called David Wallace who stated that he had come on duty at 6.5 am that Saturday morning to drive the *Parly* local train from Carlisle to Beattock. He had been an engine driver for seventeen years, he said, and when his train had arrived at Quintinshill that morning he had seen that the down loop had been occupied and that the coal empties train had been standing at the home signal about to draw into the up loop.

His fireman had gone to the signal box and had told him when he had returned that they were to be kept on the up line until the second of the two London expresses had passed. He described how Hutchinson had looked up and seen the signals for the up line lying off and how he had drawn his attention to them, but then they had both seen the troop train a mere two hundred yards away and bearing down fast.

He told the Inspector that he had observed fire immediately after the first collision; it had broken out amid the wreckage of the troop train, just behind the engine.

'What caused the fire?' asked Druitt.

'I think it would be the gas that was really the cause of the fire,' replied the engine driver, and this drew a mutter from some of the Caledonian officials.

'It was not caused by ashes from the engine?' queried the Inspector.

'I did not see any fire from the engine,' said Wallace emphatically. 'In view of the position in which the engine was lying, it would be practically impossible for any fire to have come from it.'

Driver Wallace gave this evidence with some deliberation but this wasn't at all what the railway authorities wanted to hear. His evidence contradicted that of Driver Moss who had implied that the fire had been started by hot cinders from one of the engines of the express. Moreover, Wallace had been closer to the seat of the fire when it had broken out

Whether or not burning coals or hot cinders spilled from the firebars of one or more of the engines involved, it does appear that the fire had more than one seat and that fire broke out, more or less at the same time, in several places along the wreckage. This could only have happened if gas was at least partly to blame.

For a long time the Railway Inspectorate had warned against the use of gas to light trains and a tragic railway accident at Ais Gill - only two years before and just twenty miles from Carlisle where two gas lit trains had collided with the wreck subsequently catching fire - had served as yet another warning about the danger of gas in railway carriages.

But still the use of gas persisted, although it was being phased out. Had it not been for the war this process would have been faster. All new vehicles were now built with electric lighting.

The Inspector proceeded to call the other railwaymen who had been involved and they told how they had fought the fire and rescued passengers from the wreckage. Guard Graham of the *Parly* told the inquiry how he had run back down the line, after recovering from the fall that had stunned him momentarily, to warn the oncoming express. Benson and Grierson, the footplate men from the coal empties train, told of how they had done likewise. The drivers of the two engines from the express confirmed that

they had seen Guard Graham and had immediately applied
their brakes.

FORTY-ONE

There was nothing much to excite the inquiry until the Inspector called George Hutchinson to the stand, the fireman of the local train. He had gone to the signal box, he said, when his train had arrived at Quintinshill and reversed on to the up line, as he was required to do under Rule 55 of the code governing the conduct of railway operations. This stated that the fireman of a train shunted to an opposite running line should report its presence there to the signalman in charge and should sign his name in the train register book to witness this fact. He should also ensure that any safety devices - such a lever collars - had been properly employed.

Hutchinson confirmed to the Inspector that he had gone to the box and signed his name.

'Should you have seen that the collar was on the lever of the up home signal?' asked the Inspector rhetorically.

'Yes.'

'Did you do that'

'No' replied the fireman.

Mr Lightfoot, the NUR solicitor then stepped in to see whether he might mitigate this rather damning admission and in response Hutchinson said that he had not thought it necessary to see that a collar had been placed on the signal as Tinsley, having travelled with him on the engine, ought to have known quite well where it was.

The Inspector asked Hutchinson to stand down and called one of the soldiers from the troop train - Lieutenant Bell of the 7th Royal Scots - who had been injured in the collision and appeared before the inquiry with his head and his hand in bandages. Bell said he had been travelling in the third compartment of the first coach and asleep at the time of the accident. He was awakened, he said, by what he described as a 'slight shock' and had found himself falling down with glass and water all about. A space followed before the second shock which he characterised as also very slight, and then he had been able to clamber out of the wreckage without too much difficulty. He said he had not noticed any fire at first.

His evidence illustrated the curiously uneven pattern of forces which had acted on the troop train in the moment of collision: the telescoping of some parts of the train acting as a cushion for other parts. Some soldiers were thus able to escape practically unscathed (though many, like Lieut. Bell himself, were subsequently to be injured during the rescue), while colleagues sitting next to them or in adjacent compartments had been mangled or killed.

Robert Killin, the Caledonian's assistant superintendent of the line, was next called to make a statement on behalf of the Company. He told the Inspector that he had already made some inquiry into the circumstances connected with the accident and had discovered the irregular way in which the signalmen were in the habit of changing shifts. He said that 6 am was the hour laid down by the Company as the proper time for the handover and that as Alexander Thorburn, the Gretna stationmaster, under whose direct supervision the signalmen came, was not aware of their irregular practice, the higher officials of the Company were necessarily ignorant of it too.

He pointed out that changing duty other than at the authorised time was contrary to the Company's rules and regulations and that the stationmaster was required to visit the signal box to inspect its working as frequently as his other duties permitted. There was also a district inspector on the southern portion of the railway who had three assistants and these, too, visited the signal box at irregular intervals to monitor the working. The box had been last inspected on 19th May, three days before the accident, when an assistant had visited it twice. Three other visits had taken place the previous month.

Killin gave his view quite clearly that the signalman who had shunted the local train to the up line should have completed the signalling for it; he should have given the 'blocking back' signal, keeping the indicator lock on the whole time. If the other signalman had taken over, he said, then the signalman initiating the movement should have personally satisfied himself that the safety precautions had been taken.

This evidence was damning to Meakin and he must have left the County Hall considerably more anxious than when he had first attended in the morning.

The Inspector closed the inquiry at 4.15 and retired to consider his report, remarking that if it were necessary to take more evidence, he would give notice.

But there was no need. The material facts were simple - indeed the simplicity of the primary cause seemed to obscure all the secondary issues that might have been investigated. Thus there was no real attempt to consider the extent to which gas lighting in the troop train contributed to the tragedy; and no investigation at all of the tardy reaction of the Carlisle Fire Brigade.

Neither was there any serious attempt to assess the relative severity of the two collisions, nor to reach a definite conclusion about the time that elapsed between them. In the focus on the irregular changeover in the signalmens' shifts and the failure to employ the required safety mechanisms - the blocking back signal and placing lever collars on the signal handles - the opportunity to address the problem of safety where - as in this case - there were not one but two trains on a line, was missed.

All these secondary issues were submerged behind an understandable welter of public indignation at the disaster and a desire to portray culpability in the starkest possible terms.

FORTY - TWO

In the days that followed Colonel Druitt's enquiry a rumour began to circulate in Carlisle to the effect that the signalmen had been arrested. This Donald Matheson, the Caledonian's General Manager, was at pains to deny, pointing out that the two men had only been suspended while inquiries were being conducted into the cause of the accident, though he must have known that there would be precious little chance of their ever being re-instated.

Chief Constable Gordon of the Dumfries-shire police force was at pains to deny the rumour, too, telling the local press that it was only fair to Meakin and Tinsley that no such untruth be allowed to spread. No arrests had been made, he said, and he had no orders to arrest anyone. Nevertheless, the rumours persisted and the Chief Constable knew that it was only a matter of time before the Crown took steps to proceed against one, and possibly both, signalmen.

Early on the Saturday, precisely seven days after the accident, the Chief Constable's orders came through. They were to arrest James Tinsley, the man who had pulled the fatal signal levers.

Tinsley was arrested at his home in the railway cottage beside the line at Gretna and it was the Chief Constable himself who made the arrest. Intelligence about Tinsley's distressed state had already reached him and in view of the public interest, it seems Chief Constable Gordon preferred to do the arresting himself. As a precaution he took with him Dr Maxwell Ross, the County Medical Officer, and travelled not in a police car, but in an ambulance.

Whatever Tinsley's mental state at Gretna it was even worse by the time the motor ambulance reached Dumfries. By then he had become so weak that he couldn't stand unaided and had to be assisted from the vehicle and half-dragged up the steps into the Sheriff's Court in Buccleugh Street. With Dr Ross standing close by him, Sheriff Campion charged him with culpable homicide.

The hearing lasted only a few minutes during which Tinsley collapsed and had to be led away with tears running down his cheeks to spend what remained of the weekend in Dumfries prison.

Neither did his mental state improve there. After the agonised week of waiting for the inevitable knock on the door that would spell the end of his career and the family's income, the shock of a cell door slamming shut and the key grating in the lock became too much for him and he again collapsed. His body shivered compulsively and he sobbed loudly in uncontrollable bursts. A doctor diagnosed nervous breakdown and they took him away to the more comfortable surroundings of the prison hospital.

He didn't stay there long for on the Monday morning Mr Lightfoot, the solicitor employed by the National Union of Railwaymen, arranged bail for him in the sum of £50, which the Union guaranteed and early that afternoon, when his wife visited him in the prison, they told him he could depart. Tinsley and his wife were just in time to catch the 3.15 train from Dumfries to Lockerbie and by Monday night he was back in his railway cottage at Gretna, though he must have wondered just how long the family would be able to go on living there.

While Tinsley had been in Dumfries prison, on that Sunday, 'more than 10,000' people had gathered on the Links in Leith in response to numerous advertisements for a massive recruiting meeting. They came to show their sympathy with the relatives of the men killed or injured in the railway disaster but the main object was to hear stirring recruiting speeches that told the men of Leith to 'face the next duty - to fill up the empty ranks of the 7th Royal Scots.'

And after the silent sorrow of the funeral processions, it was a way for the town's anger at the disaster to be expressed in patriotism and directed against the Germans. Two platforms had been set up and from each speakers, without the benefit of microphones, addressed the crowds.

Our view of the battles of the First War is one of senseless slaughter, of carnage on an industrial scale. It seems to us a futile struggle with precious little point. But in that first year of war those in charge of sending the armies to the front saw matters very differently. The Reverend Wallace Williamson, chaplain to the 1st Lowland Brigade spoke of the struggle against the forces of evil in which Britain was engaged. Scotland would go the way of Belgium, he surmised, unless men came forward to defend her; and her beauty and the life and liberty which she contained would be drained away. He quoted Walter Scott who had written 'who would not die for such a land?'

He appealed now to the young men in his audience to step where the Gretna men had stood and giving his opinion that it was God's will that they should. Other speakers said that the grandest monument they could raise to those who perished would be a living one. The Allied armies in France were making progress, but on present rates it would take another 25 years to reach the Rhine. More men were needed now; indeed ten men were needed for every one who had died.

The meeting continued; each speaker pointing to the dangers that the nation faced and the need to arm fully against them. For two hours they cajoled and persuaded and browbeat and appealed to the better instincts of the crowd to step forward and to take the King's shilling and many did so there and then.

Eventually, it was all over. The crowds sang the National Anthem and, led by Provost Malcolm Smith, gave three hearty cheers for the King. Then, in the early evening, they drifted away over the Links to their homes, hoping no doubt that the war would be soon over and that it really wouldn't take 25 years to bring a conclusion.

FORTY-THREE

The week before this recruiting meeting, at just about the same time on the Sunday evening that the Caledonian Railway's gangers finished relaying the line at Quintinshill, the *Empress of Britain* slipped her moorings and set sail from Liverpool carrying the 4th battalion of the Royal Scots and the remaining two companies, B and C of the 7th.

She also carried Lieutenant-Colonel Peebles and the five other officers who had come uninjured through the Gretna disaster. Assisted by tugs, the mail steamer made her way slowly out along the Mersey before turning south into the Irish Sea and heading for Land's End and the South West Approaches.

Most of the young territorials had never been on board a ship in full sea before and sea-sickness soon began to sap at their energy and enthusiasm. But otherwise the voyage was uneventful and as they sailed south into the Bay of Biscay and the men began to find their sea legs, the weather became warm. A day or so later they were passing through the Straits of Gibraltar and, with Africa on one side of them and southern Europe on the other, began to experience the fierce heat of the Mediterranean.

After a week at sea they stopped at Malta to take on fresh water and for many of the troops it was their first experience of going ashore on foreign soil. But they had soon to re-embark for they were off again, cruising through the blue water of the eastern Mediterranean until the coast of Africa loomed once again on the starboard bow. The coast grew closer and the word spread that they would disembark at Alexandria. On Thursday 3 June the *Empress of Britain* docked at this mouth of the Nile.

Once ashore the soldiers from the damp and cold shores of the Forth were met by the savage Egyptian sun, the heat and light rose off the sandy roadways until it half-blinded their eyes. They could feel the heat, the soldiers said in their letters home, even through the soles of their boots as they marched westwards, out of Alexandria and towards Aboukir, a few miles distant. There they set out their tents and ate a meal trying to keep both flies and sand out of their food.

'*All I can say about Egypt*' wrote one of the 7th Royal Scots to his parents back in Leith, '*is that it is a land where there is too much of some things and too little of others.. Every creature that can creep, crawl or fly and give the greatest amount of annoyance to human beings, makes this part of the globe its earthly paradise. My sincerest sympathy goes out to the ancient ruler of this country who suffered from a plague of flies. When you see a thing like a submarine on wings making straight for you*

it makes you wonder what you had for tea. Scorpions in
your pockets and snakes under your bed in the morning
are only a few of the trials and tribulations of life out here.
The animals would be all right if they didn't bite. The
snakes, fortunately are not of a very deadly type.'

But the Royal Scots had little time to become
habituated to their surroundings for five days later they
wrapped up their tents and set out on the road again,
marching back to Alexandria and the *Empress of Britain*
for the final voyage to Turkish shores and whatever might
await them in Gallipoli. On the *Empress of Britain* they
might find themselves again cramped and confined but at
least they were free of sand and flies.

For 600 miles the white painted steamer chugged her
way through the blue seas; past the green shores of Crete
and then north through the Aegean heading towards the
Dardanelles. For the troops these were halcyon days of
calm before the storm of a war which fortunately few of
them could even imagine.

The officers arranged routines and exercises to keep
the troops engaged and Captain Wightman, one of the
officers who had escaped injury at Gretna, called for
volunteers to man a new signal section to replace the one
which, had been lost in the rail disaster. Soon these
volunteers were running back and forth along the decks of
the *Empress of Britain*, trailing reels of signal wire and
telephoning each other from opposite ends of the ship.
They learned and practised the codes and ciphers and
studied the signal books, which Captain Wightman

otherwise kept under lock and key. Despite the distractions of the voyage, he was well pleased with their progress.

By Friday, June 11th they had reached the port of Mudros, on the island of Lemnos, just 50 miles from Gallipoli. This was as far as the *Empress of Britain* would be taking them. Again the 4th Royal Scots and the two remaining companies of the 7th battalion disembarked and together they unloaded all the brigade's stores. These they transferred to an old and rusty freighter - a small ship without accommodation called the *Carron*. This was the ship that would ferry them from Mudros to the Gallipoli beaches.

This work took all day and in the dying rays of the sun, after they had eaten, they reflected on this, their last night of tranquility. The voyage, for those who had never before been more than a few miles from their homes, had been one of great excitement, but also, cramped and confined as they had been, with little to do or to read or to entertain them, it had been a voyage of great boredom as well. They looked forward uncertainly to what might await them on the hills of the Dardanelles hidden behind the heat haze on the eastern horizon. They remembered what they had read in the newspaper accounts when they first went into training in Larbert: of the valour of the troops and the blood that had been shed during the first landings. They wouldn't be facing that, they hoped.

Still many lay awake, smoking or looking up at the stars, feeling as all soldiers must do the night before a battle, a mixture of anticipation tinged with gloom and regret; of eagerness mixed with resignation. What will be will be. When they spoke, they talked cheerfully and boasted to keep their spirits high, yet all had their own inner doubts: would they, too, behave honourably or would they flinch in face of the Turkish machine guns? Would they disgrace themselves and crack before their comrades? Their palms became sweaty long before they drifted into a turbulent and interrupted sleep.

By the middle of the following day all the soldiers had embarked on the crowded *Carron* and the crew had cast her off from the quay. The steamer chugged out of the harbour and set course for Gallipoli, the white-washed cottages of Lemnos and the island's pine clad hills, slowly retreating into the distance. The soldiers' destination was only a few hours away but as yet the 1,500 Royal Scots could make nothing out on the eastern horizon. Soon, however, they were in Turkish waters. On the port bow, some ten miles distant, they caught their first sight of Turkey in the shape of the substantial island of Imroz. And then, straight ahead and rising through the heat haze they saw the darkening smudge of the horizon that was their destination.

Though they didn't know then that they saw was the hill known as *Achi Baba*, at 650 feet the highest point on the ridge that formed the spine of the Gallipoli peninsular. The men crowded forward for a first glimpse of the land that most would never leave uninjured and which half of them would never leave at all.

The plan had been for the troops to arrive and disembark under cover of darkness but somehow this had not been communicated to the *Carron's* captain for the ship arrived off *Cape Helles* - the most southerly point of the peninsular - disconcertingly early. At seven o'clock, the twilight had not even begun to thicken and the sun was still a red ball in the western sky. Disembarkation under the shadow of the Turkish guns on the hill would be hazardous enough and even more so without the relative safety darkness. So the *Carron* dropped her anchor about two miles off shore, just out of range of those guns, the cables rattling out over her rust-pitted sides. As the Royal Scots, eager to get into action, endured yet another forced wait, they might have reflected that they were, of course, a sitting duck should a Turkish submarine be lurking. It would also be a simple matter for the Turks to call in an aeroplane - if they had one in service - to drop grenades into the freighter packed with 1,500 British soldiers.

But it appeared that Turkey had no serviceable aeroplanes on the Gallipoli peninsular that evening and if the Turkish submarine that had successfully sent the British Cruiser HMS Triumph to the bottom just a few months before, was in service then it wasn't in the vicinity. Sitting calmly in the blue sea, on a summer's evening, packed with troops, *Carron* was neither torpedoed nor bombed and as night fell she moved inshore and remarkably the troops were able to disembark safely on 'V' beach at Cape Helles without losing a single man. From there they were directed to a rest camp.

FORTY-FOUR

When the next day the Royal Scots had an opportunity to take their bearings, they saw the beaches where the first Gallipoli landings had been made and reckoned they had been lucky not to have found themselves in that first wave. Looking at the sheer cliffs all around they thought the beaches ought to have been impregnable, as indeed they almost were. In the so-called rest camp the soldiers also came under fire for the first time. Described as a rabbit warren big enough to hold thousands of troops - it was not secure or safe from shelling by the Turkish guns and occasional bursts of shrapnel fell on the camp at intervals.

From here Colonel Peebles penned a letter home to Scotland with a description of what his troops were facing.

'The peninsular is a sandy, undulating piece of country with two roads leading north-east. There is a little vegetation, but mostly scrub. It is broiling hot during the day but cools down during the evening. The flies are terrible, and prevent sleep or rest during the day, and the amount of sand that we eat, drink and breathe is enormous!

'The Straits are not very wide and the Asiatic coast with a high range of hills is seen to the east while to the west and south-west are the islands of Imbros and Tenedos. We have beautiful sun and moon effects morning and night, and at times the scene towards Imbros reminds one of the West Coast of Scotland looking towards Arran (I wish it were). We have had rain for ten minutes since leaving home.

'The Turks hold the hill called Achi Baba (650 feet), which has command of the whole place, and until we drive them back from it they have a distinct advantage. Our losses have been heavy but they are nothing to what the Turks have lost, and I think the best troops they had are gone. But, of course, trench warfare is bound to be slow and equalises very much the difference between good and indifferent troops, especially when the latter are on the defensive.'

Here he was only too right as the Royal Scots were soon to discover for themselves, but for the moment they were all employed on digging divisional dugouts and in working on the mass of reserve and communication trenches which covered the face of the peninsular. Since the initial landings in April, the Allies had advanced some four or five miles, so that the front now stretched in a diagonal line across the peninsular from the north-west to the south-east.

Because the whole of this ground was in range of the Turkish guns on the Achi Baba ridge, all communication and travel had to be through the narrow, congested communications trenches and the Royal Scots thought that this movement, to and fro between the dugout rest camp and the front lines, was the most trying part of their day. It could take several hours to march up to the front line carrying picks and shovels, pushing and shoving their way past other soldiers and all under the fierce heat of the summer sun. Uniforms were now quickly discarded for dried sweat stiffened the khaki cloth making it hard as cardboard and chaffing the angles of their bodies.

There were other discomforts, too, for the Turkish guns made satisfactory sanitary arrangements almost impossible. Besides there was no freshwater available on the peninsular: all water for the allied soldiers had to be brought in by sea under fire. What this meant was that only rarely could the men in the trenches be afforded the luxury of a wash. Their greatest joy when in the rest camp by the beach was to swim in the clear blue sea, bathing the sores on their bodies. But even in the sea there was no respite from the occasional Turkish shell and the men used to think that they were safer sometimes in the front line where the proximity of their own men made the Turkish gunners wary of trying to shell them.

One Leith territorial wrote home:

'This is being written in the firing line. Life here is pretty primitive. I don't think you would recognise me if you saw me with a few days growth on my chin, face unwashed, trousers cut into shorts, a cap comforter and sleeves rolled up. There you have a mixture of boy scout, a

navvy, tramp and a soldier. We are indeed a picturesque lot. One look at us and the enemy would bolt - that is if he had any sense. The firing line is about the most secure spot in this place. Every other part of the line is within range of shell fire. Our friends facing us are such indifferent artillerymen that they cannot shell us without damaging themselves. Needless to say we are very grateful for this defect on the enemy's part. Shell fire is no picnic.

'We have to cook our own food. The substantial part is brought to us in tins, while the next consists of tea, mostly stewed, biscuits and jam with an occasional loaf of bread. To vary the monotony of diet we may now and then get a mouthful of flies. You have to carry your food to your mouth in a zig-zag course just in an attempt to dodge these troublesome insects. This place would break the heart of any 'kill that fly' enthusiast. Snipers and flies are our only trouble during the day. If you keep you head well down there is nothing to fear from bullets.

'Our hardest work takes place from dusk to dawn. By way of a truce to keep up our spirits we take hour about in keeping watch and sleep is impossible. But we endeavour to make up for this during the day when things are easier.'

What such letters omitted was any reference to the noxious smell of Gallipoli. The odour of thousands of unwashed troops toiling and sweating in the hot sun must have been singularly unpleasant, but it was compounded many times by the smell of ordure and, even more strongly, the stench of death. For Gallipoli was one great

256

charnel house, the dead lying unburied for long stretches. It was almost as though Gallipoli was a battle fought not primarily with guns and bullets but with noxious miasmas.

The Turks did not concern themselves at all with sanitation and while the Allied dead were buried as soon as practically possible, many of the Turkish dead were left unburied wherever they fell. Indeed they were even put to practical use as bullet stoppers and piled in heaps along the parapets of the trenches in which they had served, cemented together with a thin layer of clay. British troops capturing a Turkish trench would sometimes find scores of bodies half-mummified in this way. Other bodies became trodden into the floor of a trench from where the remains of arms and legs would protrude at grotesque angles.

Little wonder that the flies had a field day and with so many bodies left unburied, disease hung in the air so that the peninsular became one huge lazar house in which sickness spread terrifyingly fast. Very few soldiers remained free from an energy sapping stomach or bowel disorder and serious cases had to be invalided home.

Faced with these adversities the Royal Scots remained in good heart despite taking a few casualties from the sporadic shelling. One man, detailed to water the mules used to transport the battalion's stores, had been killed in this way while attending to the animals, a few others had been wounded, but to all intents and purposes the 4th battalion and the 7th half battalion were considered fresh troops and quite ready for a renewal of the Allied offensive.

FORTY-FIVE

Meanwhile, back in London, in the Whitehall Offices of the Board of Trade, Lieutenant-Colonel Druitt dated his report of the Quintinshill accident 17th June 1915 and addressed it to the Assistant Secretary at the Railway Department. It was 24 pages long with three pages of appendices and most were taken up with the condensed transcripts of the evidence taken at Carlisle; the factual details of the trains involved and with the times and speeds and distances and other factors that the Inspector thought relevant. He also quoted extracts from the Code for Signalbox Operations, published in April 1912 by Thomas Pettigrew, the Caledonian's General Superintendent of the Line, focusing in particular on the section describing the use of lever collars. In an appendix he gave the final, awful, tally of casualties, insofar as this could ever be accurately ascertained: 227 dead and 246 injured.

Druitt described the late running of the London expresses and the despatch of the local train ahead of them. He wrote of the actions of Meakin and Tinsley in the signal cabin, but offered no opinion as to which of them had given the fatal 'train out of section' signal for the coal empties train at 6.34. He went on to describe the collisions and the fires that followed and the attempts of Graham, Benson and Grierson to warn the express. The men's movements had been reconstructed later and timed with a stopwatch, Druitt reported.

'The times recorded varied a good deal, but as Benson and Grierson......and D. Graham.....were the only men who ran back and as Driver Johnstone of the train engine corroborates the positions they said they had reached, their times are probably the most reliable. It was found that Benson and his fireman were 132 and 147 yards, respectively, from their engine, and Graham 167 yards from where he left his van, when the 6.5 am express passed them, and the time taken was 31 seconds for Benson and 40 seconds for Graham.......Graham got the furthest and was 278 yards from the point of the second collision or about 170 yards outside the home signal.

'Driver Cowper of the leading engine of the 6.5 express says both distant and home signals were off for him (when) his foreman shouted to him that something was wrong,........He saw at the same time that he had just passed the guard of the local train. He places this point as between the underbridge south of the signal box and the buffer stops of the down loop. Half way between these two points is 163 yards outside the home signal, or only about 7 yards from where Guard Graham says he got to.'

Druitt calculated that the express had taken 40 seconds to run from the distant signal to the point of the second collision and he concluded from this that *'if*

Graham's time was correct then there was an interval of 53 seconds between the time he left his van after being knocked down in the first collision, and the second collision, and so it is quite possible that had the down distant signal been thrown to danger at once when the first collision occurred it would have been against the 6.5 am express before the latter reached it. But, of course,........it is impossible to be positive. It is certain, however, that the down signals were not thrown to danger immediately after the first collision occurred.'

But the Inspector took no account of the time Graham had lain stunned in his van and for the time it had taken him then to come to and remember the express. An extra 15 seconds here would have seemed a conservative estimate. That would make 58 seconds, and would suggest that the London express could well have been 18 seconds, or some 500 yards, outside the distant signal, at the time of the first collision.

This is borne out by an estimate of the time it would have taken Meakin to run back up the signal box steps after the first collision, remonstrate with Tinsley, enquire as to the position of the London express and then throw over the down distant signal lever. A time of 20 seconds here does not seem unrealistic. If the express had been 500 yards outside the distant signal at the time of the first collision then a 20 second delay would have meant that the drivers of the express would have been already past the distant signal when it was thrown to danger. Yet had, as Druitt suggested, the down distant signal been thrown to danger immediately, then almost certainly the second collision would have been averted.

The report turned to the cause of the accident and here Druitt was emphatic.

'The responsibility for the collision lies entirely with the two signalmen......as all signals were lowered for the troop train at the time of the first collision, and for the express. Meakin crossed the 6.10 local train from the down to the up line, and it was unquestionably his duty to have protected it, both by sending the 'Blocking Back' signal to Kirkpatrick and also by placing a clip on the up home signal lever, before handing over his duties to Tinsley. He should also have given the 'out of section' signal to Kirkpatrick for the empty wagon train, which he had placed in the up loop line (as he had done all other signalling in connection with it) as soon as he replaced the points and the up loop home signal.

'Tinsley should also have seen that the 6.10 local train was properly protected, as he was fully aware that it was standing on the up line, but his attention was probably taken up by making the numerous entries in the Register, and also in dealing with the signalling of the two expresses; so when he was offered the troop train at 6.42, he at once accepted it on the block instrument, which was in the normal position and not locked as it should have been. Having got the troop train accepted by Gretna Junction at 6.46, he lowered all his signals for it, forgetting all about the 6.10 am local train, which was *standing only 62 yards away from the centre of the signal box.'*

But it was not only the signalmen who came in for criticism.

'Hutchinson......came to the signal box to carry out Rule 55, and signed his name in the Register in accordance with the instructions. Tinsley saw him do this, but although Hutchinson remained in the cabin some four minutes before returning to his engine he neglected to get an assurance from Tinsley that his train was protected by a collar being placed on the lever of the up home signal, as he should have done.'

Druitt concluded with what he saw to be the nub of the argument.

'Men engaged in routine work, where the conditions may easily become dangerous either to themselves or to others, sometimes get into a loose way of working, and habitually neglect regulations which have been laid down for their own or others protection. I have noticed in other cases that the use of the lever collar has been neglected, and both Meakin and Tinsley admitted that they did not think it necessary to use one to protect a train crossed over from one line to the other, and that it was seldom used.

'This disastrous collision was thus due to want of discipline on the part of the signalmen, first by changing duty at an unauthorised hour, which caused Tinsley to be occupied in writing up the Train Register Book, and so diverted his attention from his proper work; secondly by Meakin handing over his duty in a very lax manner; and,

thirdly, by both signalmen neglecting to carry out various rules specially framed for preventing accidents due to forgetfulness on the part of signalmen.

'Also, it is much to be regretted, that some signalmen do not look out of the signal boxes to see if the line over which an approaching train is to run is clear of any obstacle before lowering the signals. It takes only a brief interval to do so, and many collisions could be prevented if this simple precaution was always taken. Had Tinsley looked along the line on this occasion, he could not have helped seeing the 6.10 local train standing only a short distance away.'

The fire, Inspector Druitt considered, was due primarily to live coals spilling from the overturned engine of the troop train and afterwards intensified by the escape of gas from cylinders as they burst. But he did not say how those live coals could have started so many fires simultaneously. The Inspector commented that fire would have occurred even if the coaches had been electrically lit, but he did renew the Department's earlier advice to the railway companies to the effect that *'gas lighting in existing stock be abolished....as opportunity admits..'* although he recognised that this would be a slow process spread over many years. The opportunity to make a bold attack on the use of gas in trains was therefore missed. On the other hand when the war was stretching railway companies as never before, the Inspector no doubt did not wish to add to their burdens at a time when all their energies were needed to transport troops and equipment.

The Inspector made no investigation of, nor did he comment upon, the delayed arrival of the fire brigade; perhaps he did not consider this his job, but had the brigade arrived even an hour earlier a considerably greater number of lives might have been saved.

FORTY-SIX

Quintinshill remains to this day the worst disaster ever to have taken place upon a British railway. The only previous comparable accident had been the runaway train of Armagh which had killed 80 and injured 400 in 1889. The worst accident in Scotland had been the Tay Bridge disaster of 1879 when 75 had died. In more recent times, the scale of the Quintinshill disaster has only once been approached by the accident at Harrow and Wealdstone station in October 1952 when 112 lives were lost.

Although the disaster took place a mile and a half inside Scotland, many of those who succumbed to their injuries died in England having been removed to hospital in Carlisle. They included James Ferguson Macdonald, the golfer from the express who had lost two of his fingers in the rescue, and sustained other injuries as well. Besides him, 26 more of the injured had died in Carlisle hospitals. As there was uncertainty as to the exact cause of their deaths, English law required the local Coroner to hold an inquest.

A month had now passed since Coroner T. S. Strong had formally opened the inquest on the Tuesday following the accident and since that time five more of the Royal Scots had died. It was time now for the adjourned inquest to proceed. Having sworn in a 19 member jury, the Coroner took them to the scene of the accident. The Caledonian laid on a special train and there in the signal box Robert Killin explained to them the workings of the block instruments and the signals that had to be given and recorded in order that trains might pass.

Dr Edwards, the young rugby playing surgeon, gave evidence to identify the dead among whom lay Private Clark whose leg he had amputated among the gas cylinders and where it had been so hot that the chloroform mask he had used had ignited before he could apply it to his patient.

As at Druitt's inquiry the railwaymen gave their evidence and their accounts did not differ from those they had given to the Inspector. Meakin and Tinsley had in fact been asked whether they wished to give evidence that might possibly incriminate them; they would have had the right to remain silent, but both chose to speak. Fireman Hutchinson was cautioned, too, for as Coroner Strong told the jury accurately in his summing up *'if this man had done his duty the accident would not have arisen because the lever collar would have been on.'*

Coroner Strong began by reading out large sections of the Rule Book governing railway operations and he asked the signalmen whether they were familiar with them; they said they were.

Meakin now said something that he hadn't told the Inspector which was that he expected that Tinsley would send the local train forward in the fifteen minute interval between the two London expresses, but Tinsley was not questioned about this. For his part he again admitted that he had had a lapse of memory - he had forgotten that the local train had been on the up line - and that when he pulled off his signals for the troop train the block instrument had been showing clear.

The taking of evidence lasted a day and a half for the Coroner was a persistent questioner, though with a tendency to force complicated matters into a framework of black or white. The transcript shows that he was also prone to be dismissive and to patronise some of his humbler witnesses.

Nevertheless his summing up was careful even if he presented the issues in the starkest terms. He concluded that Meakin had had a clear duty to use the lever collar and to 'block back' in respect of the local train. He said that if Tinsley had taken over during these operations then Meakin should still have personally ensured that these precautions had been taken.

'There is this to be said for Tinsley' he continued, *'that if the secondary precautions - the blocking back signal and the lever collar - had been made use of, he could not have caused the accident as he did. On the other hand his part in the matter is so glaring, that it is*

difficult to see what excuse there can be for him. *But you must be fair,'* he told the jury, *'and view his conduct in every possible light.'*

He concluded by advising the jury on the form of their verdict.

'If you find as a result of your deliberations that the rules and safeguards have been broken by one or more of the railwaymen concerned, or in other words, that there has been negligence, there remains one other point which you must decide, and it is this: is this negligence of such a character - having regard to all the surroundings - as to be culpable negligence, or in other words gross negligence? If so it is manslaughter.

'Now the term 'gross negligence' to a lay mind is apt to be misunderstood. There is no particular virtue in the word 'gross,' there is no technicality or catch about it in any way which need give you the slightest trouble. It simply means great negligence, or, to put it at the highest, very great negligence, and as plain men what you must ask each other is this. Could there be any greater negligence on the part of railwaymen than to disobey explicit rules which are a vital part of this important system - a system which any ordinary man must know is framed to protect your fellow subjects from a death such as is presented in your minds in this disaster. The rules are expressly designed for that very purpose. You will however be careful to take separately each man's case and consider what rule he has broken and whether his own particular

breach of duty amounts to gross negligence in the sense I have indicated.

'As to the form of your verdict there can only be two alternatives and I will not puzzle you by submitting to you any elaborate series of questions: they are unnecessary. the alternatives are, first, accidental death without culpable blame against anybody; and, secondly, manslaughter against one or more of the men concerned. Some of you may think that the importance of this inquiry demands that you should add recommendations by way of rider - for instance as to the use of gas in the trains - and no doubt other suggestions may occur to you, but your duties are sufficiently grave without making them more so, and personally I should advise you to leave all these subsidiary matters to the Board of Trade to whose province they belong, and to confine yourself to the main and grave issue, which is really before you.'

The jury retired to consider their verdict at 12.40 and 55 minutes elapsed before Mr Telford, their foreman led them back.

'We find,' he said, 'that these several persons met their deaths through an accident to the train in which they were travelling, which accident was caused by the gross negligence of Meakin and Tinsley and fireman Hutchinson.'

'Then that is a verdict of manslaughter against three persons,' said Coroner Strong.

A juryman sought clarification: 'I suppose twelve are sufficient for a verdict because seven of us are against the verdict in the latter case of Hutchinson and twelve are in favour of it?'

'Twelve are sufficient,' confirmed Mr Strong.

Mr Lightfoot, again appointed by the Union to defend the interests of the railwaymen now protested at the implications of the verdict. If the men had committed a criminal act, he said, then they had done this in Scotland. Tinsley had already been arrested for manslaughter and therefore could not now be re-arrested a second time on the warrant of an English court. The Coroner did not have the power to act on the jury's verdict.

But Coroner Strong, perceiving that just such a difficulty might arise from the separate legal jurisdictions of England and Scotland, had taken the precaution of consulting the Home Office beforehand. They had told him unequivocally to go ahead. He therefore thanked Mr Lightfoot and committed all three railwaymen to the next Cumberland Assizes. There would be no difficulty about Tinsley's arrest for he proposed to admit all three to bail.

However, before the Cumberland Assizes next met, there took place a session of the High Court of Judiciary in Edinburgh and, between them, the Home Office and the Scottish authorities decided that the three railwaymen might as well be tried there.

FORTY-SEVEN

Meanwhile, in Gallipoli, the Royal Scots were preparing for the offensive for which they and other troops had been sent from Britain. The attack would begin 28 June.

Since the original landings the Allied forces had advanced some four or five miles from the tip of the Gallipoli peninsular and the front line ran now diagonally - more progress having been made on the western (European) side than on the east. A major offensive by British troops on 4th June in the centre of the line had advanced the front almost a thousand yards and this had created an outward bulge whose flanks were now vulnerable to Turkish counterattack and along which skirmishes constantly took place. To reinforce the position an attack by French forces in mid June had pushed the right (eastern) side of the Allied line forward and this had brought some respite from attacks on that side, but the left (western) sector had remained exposed and on this side the new British lines were in some places no more than a few yards from the Turkish trenches. By day the British forces would bomb the Turks out of these trenches in short bloody struggles; but by night the Turks would make desperate and vicious counter-attacks.

To relieve the pressure on these trenches and also to force his way further up the peninsular, General Sir Ian Hamilton, commanding the Mediterranean Expeditionary Force, decided to mount a major attack on the left of the Allied line and it was in this attack that the remaining companies of the 7th Royal Scots were to be committed.

Facing the left of the line a dry sandy river bed, called by the British *'Krithia Nullah,'* snaked its way up the peninsula for a distance of some four miles before turning to the east and losing itself among the ravines at the foot of the Achi Baba ridge. Between the Nullah and the western coast of the peninsular lay a plateau of land about half a mile across, which had been named the *'Worcester Flats.'* Turkish defensive trenches ran all the way from the steep four hundred foot high cliffs of the coast across these flats and on down across the Nullah and then up the other side to the Achi Baba ridge.

The plan of attack was that one brigade should take and hold the Worcester flats, driving the Turks out of their trenches there while a second brigade would then use the flats to make a significant advance up the coast. It was these trenches on the Worcester flats that the 156th Brigade, commanded by Brigadier-General Scott Moncrieff, comprising the 4th and 7th Royal Scots and the 8th Scottish Rifles, were now ordered to take and hold protecting the flank of the 87th Brigade who had been given the task of driving the attack forward up the coast.

At the same time a third brigade would attack the Turkish lines to the east of the Nullah to deny them the opportunity of firing into the 156th's Brigades flanks.

Sunday June 27th was a glorious day according to Second Lieutenant Lyell of the 7th battalion's 'C' Company, though he himself felt anything but glorious. It may have been dysentery or some other bowel disorder for he felt 'out of sorts' and was resting with his friend and fellow subaltern Frank Thompson under an awning that he had made from waterproof sheeting. He may well have winced therefore when he received a message to say that the Company would probably be moving up to the front that afternoon and that Colonel Peebles had gone to Brigade headquarters for orders.

When Peebles returned he called a meeting of his officers and explained the plans for the coming attack. It would start the next day, Monday 28th, June, he said, and would start with an artillery bombardment, which would last from 9 am to 11 am, after which 'C' Company would lead an assault over the parapet and take two lines of Turkish trenches one after the other in a bayonet charge. 'B' Company would follow in support. Major Sanderson would lead the charge. The 7th Royal Scots would take the centre of the Brigade's line with the 4th Royal Scots on their left and the 8th Scottish Rifles on the right.

At 7.30 that Sunday evening, 'B' and 'C' Companies of the 7th Royal Scots therefore left their rabbit-warren rest camp by the sea and marched up the congested communications trenches to the front line. 'C' Company went straight into the firing line; 'B' Company into the support trench.

At the front as night fell Colonel Peebles went among his men giving them an eve of battle reassurance, telling them that they were going to be a part of the biggest charge that had ever taken place upon the Gallipoli peninsular. Then like all soldiers on the eve of battle they tried to get what sleep they could in the cramped, crowded, cold and uncomfortable conditions in the trenches.

When dawn came on that Monday morning all seemed quiet, and strangely peaceful. The sky was clear and soon the soldiers felt the warm rays of the sun driving through the clear air and chasing away the chill of the night. Lieutenant Lyell and the other officers from 'C' Company rose early and breakfasted together before checking on their men. Words of support, encouragement. When we get home......

Before nine o'clock the sun had already climbed high in the sky and a heat haze was rising from the parched battleground in front of them. The men could hear the hum of the Turkish army not far away. The nearest Turkish trench was just 150 yards in front of them. Lieutenant Lyell looked at his watch.

Promptly at 9 am the bombardment started, the most fiendish noise he had ever heard, Lyell was to say later. The officers kept their heads down. Peebles, who said he never could have imagined such a fearful row, echoed

Lyell's feelings. After half an hour even the sun's bright disc was veiled by thick clouds of dust and smoke that floated skywards. The acrid smell of cordite hung heavily in the air. It was impossible to believe that under such a barrage any Turks could have survived. It might be safe to take a quick look. Periscopes were raised.

What they saw disconcerted them mightily. The thick pall of black smoke and dust lay away to their right over the eastern side of the Nullah. Not a single shell appeared to have landed on the Turkish trenches facing them on this, the western side.

Perhaps they thought that the bombardment would switch now from the eastern side to the west, but the bombardment was slackening. It was a question, they learned later, of a shortage of shells. The 156th Brigade would have to attack without the benefit of artillery support. Moreover, the Turks would now have had a couple of hours notice of the attack.

The Royal Scots would have to charge at trenches garrisoned by soldiers whose nerves had not previously been shaken by prolonged shelling. With such support lacking, their only effective covering fire came from the battalion machine guns. But bullets could do no more than force the enemy to keep his head down until the moment of assault; they could neither smash hostile trenches nor bemuse a garrison and it was lucky that the men of the 156th Brigade did not realise then the difficult and forlorn nature of the task before them. For not only were the Turks well dug in to a defensive position, but they also had a clear superiority of firepower.

Having been given notice of the impending infantry assault and hampered by no shortage of artillery shells, the Turks launched their own artillery bombardment and this time the Turks gave no thought to the proximity of their own lines, the target was too tempting and the military need pressing. It was therefore the attackers rather than the defenders that found themselves under bombardment and many Royal Scots, closely packed into the crowded firing trenches became casualties that morning even before the attack started. It seemed a long time until zero hour.

In the firing line, sheltering as best they could, the Royal Scots prayed they would not buckle under whatever was to come and perhaps to avoid dwelling on this too much they kept up between them a nervous and light-hearted banter while shielding their ears from the din. It was as if, said Lieutenant Lyell, they were waiting for the doors to open at a theatre.

Along the line each man was now issued with an empty tin and told to strap it to his back so that it would reflect in the sun as he went over the top. It would be a signal to those behind to cease their firing.

But still it wanted forty minutes to zero hour and still the Turkish shells came in. Still the Royal Scots were taking casualties. Major Sanderson came along the line and Lyell checked his watch. Each man now cut hand and foot holds for himself in the clay of the trench; speed in clearing the parapet would be vital to his safety. Beside

Colonel Peebles, Captain Dawson passed on messages of encouragement. At 10.45 everyone was ordered to fix bayonets to their Lee-Enfield rifles and to move into position. The bayonets long since honed to perfection glinted whenever they caught the sun.

Along the lines the sergeants counted down the minutes. 'Three minutes to go, boys.' Then two, then one. To the west the artillery stopped.

FORTY-EIGHT

'Come on, boys!' Captain Dawson's shout echoed down the firing trench and the long first line of soldiers came over the parapet as one, cheering and yelling as they went. Led by Major Sanderson on the left and Captain Dawson on the right they charged into a hail of rifle and machine gun fire. As they ran the Royal Scots crouched over their rifles, as they had been told, so as to present a smaller target, even so many were dropping as the second line under Captain Torrance and Lieutenant Ballantyne came up out of the trench and tore after them. And then came the third line, under Captain Clark.

The first and second lines crossed the 150 yards of open ground and took the first Turkish trench, Lieutenant Lyell loosing off all six chambers of his revolver at the cowering Turks. Those not killed bolted under this wild onslaught of the Royal Scots. Relatively safe in the Turkish trench, Lyell re-loaded his revolver and waited while the third line came up. All around his men kept up a rapid fire forward towards the second Turkish trench some two hundred yards away.

All three lines now charged this second Turkish trench, the main Turkish defensive position and heavily fortified. The Turks had a clear field of fire at the 7th Royal Scots who were running over two hundred yards of open ground in a dense pack of almost 500 men. The Turks let fly with every arm they had; rifles and machine guns poured a constant hail of bullets into the advancing soldiers, while behind the Turkish trench their artillery laid down a pattern fire of shrapnel.

The massacre was appalling. Indeed it seemed miraculous that any of the Royal Scots could come through that terrible mixture of shell and gunfire. Long before they reached the second trench the ranks of charging soldiers became woefully thin with whole groups of men dropping together in bundles on the sun-baked ground.

Leading the charge Major Sanderson had covered perhaps fifty yards when he fell and Captain Dawson and Lieutenant Frank Thompson - a Gretna survivor - fell shortly after. Though reduced in number the awful charge ploughed on and the survivors reaching the second Turkish trench bayoneted any of the Turkish soldiers who chose not to retreat.

There for the moment the remaining Royal Scots paused while Lieutenant Haws, now the senior officer, organised the trench for defence, turning the guns around so that they would fire in the opposite direction.

Colonel Peebles had not himself taken part in the attack. He must have had doubts about whether he would be fit enough to keep up with the raging soldiers. But he watched the attack through a periscope and observed his men doing 'great execution,' driving out the Turks at bayonet point; but he also observed the casualties, men falling and sometimes crying out in agony as shrapnel or bullets tore into them.

Those that had suffered in this way now began to stream back to what was the British front line. Some were horribly injured but there were no complaints and one young soldier observing these casualties wrote home to tell his parents *'If you know of any young man who has not made his mind up yet about enlisting, tell him that if he has any manhood in him he should hesitate no longer. Not for his own sake, but for the sake of those who have suffered and died.'*

Another of the Royal Scots who had managed to make his way back to the British line, despite his injuries, wrote home to Leith from a hospital bed in Egypt.

'We jumped over the parapet and gave the charge. The Captain was shouting "Good old Seventh" when he got shot down. I got shot fighting with a couple of Turks. After I had killed them I got struck and fell down into a captured trench. When I came to myself, I happened to look round and there was a Turk aiming at me. In another second I would have been killed. I finished it by putting my bayonet in him and leaving it there. Then I crawled up on my stomach to our old trench, where I could get a chance of getting down to the hospital boat. Proceeding

there I got a bullet through my helmet; I thought my head was off. However, they just missed it and no more.'

Many of the wounded had no chance of getting themselves back to their own lines and some lay in the savage heat and dust and bled to death from their wounds or died of thirst in the fierce glare of the Gallipoli sun.

Even for those who reached the second Turkish trench alive, there was no escape from danger. Although Lieutenant Haws and Lyell soon had men organised to turn the trench around so that they could fire the Turkish guns in the right direction, the construction of a suitable parapet took longer. All the time the new position was being shelled by the Turkish artillery and Royal Scots survivors continued to take casualties.

To their left of their line the 4th Royal Scots had also achieved their objective, taking that part of the second Turkish trench that faced them. They had also taken casualties on a similar scale. However, to the right the attack by the 8th Scottish Rifles had fizzled out, drowned in a hail of machine gun fire even fiercer than that which the 7th Royal Scots had faced. The Brigade Commander, Scott-Moncrieff had himself been killed in a forlorn attempt to bring up support to these men. But the consequence was now that the right flank of the 7th Royal Scots lay completely unprotected and was now exposed to enfilading machine gun fire from the same heavy machine guns that had stopped the Scottish rifles.

FORTY-NINE

Communications were difficult in these savage, hectic hours. Captain Wightman, in the rear with his signal volunteers under the command of Sergeant Rosie, attempted to run out a telephone line from the captured trenches back to battalion headquarters, but practically every inch of the ground was under fire. Sergeant Rosie was inevitably killed and Captain Wightman, wounded in this forlorn attempt, but efforts to set up the telephone link continued until every one of the signal section had become casualties and once again the battalion (or what by then remained of it) was without a signal section.

During the rest of that momentous day small platoons of men were brought up as reinforcements but it was a long while before the position could be properly defended. Moreover, as Major Ewing would write later in his history of the Royal Scots, '*The dust and sand that filled the air clogged the rifle bolts, while the men were suffering from exhaustion and the terrific mental strain of their first fight; their mouths were so parched by heat and dust that their tongues swelled and they could scarcely swallow the rations that they had carried up; worst of all was the craving for water, and the troops endured long hours of agony before the precious liquid could be sent up to them.'*

For a time the Turks were too disorganised to be able to mount a effective counter-attack, but this situation did not last and towards evening, they in their turn charged over the shell-pocked ground at the Royal Scots in the captured trenches. But Lieutenant Elliot - another Gretna survivor - who had been attached to the 7th Royal Scots from the Highland Light Infantry was waiting for the charge with a heavy machine gun and this chattered away steadily until the water boiled in its cooling barrel and the brass cases of the spent ammunition piled up on the trench floor. He, too, was reported to have done 'great execution' that day, but eventually, perhaps because of the inadequate parapet, a sniper managed to get a bead upon him and a Turkish bullet split open his head.

Nevertheless, with new hands manning the gun, the waves of counter-attacking Turks fell back. A pause, and then they charged again, and again the machine guns clattered in the gathering dusk. And so the struggle continued until nightfall, when gradually the guns on both sides fell silent.

During the night the Royal Scots were relieved by men from the Hampshire regiment who took over the still unconsolidated position. The remnants of the 4th and 7th Royal Scots withdrew to the comparative safety of the reserve trenches.

It was time to count the cost. The 7th Royal Scots knew that they had taken terrible casualties, but when they mustered after the action, only three officers and 80 unwounded of other ranks remained. Of those who had taken part that day, eleven officers had been killed or were listed as missing in action, in addition to the 230 casualties in other ranks, of whom 116 had been killed or were missing. These casualties came from only two companies or half a battalion.

To their left the losses sustained by the 4th Royal Scots had been equally appalling; the ground between the trenches had been left thick with dead and wounded. Most of their officers, too, had fallen before the first objective had been attained, but the men had pressed on led by their NCOs and when these were also killed, the men had continued to charge and to bayonet any Turks who didn't flee. Lieutenant-Colonel Dunn, Colonel of the 4th Royal Scots had been mortally wounded in the initial stages of the attack and the battalion had lost 15 other officers killed, mortally wounded or missing. Six officers had received less serious wounds. Casualties among other ranks amounted to 345 men of which 204 were either killed or missing.

As the sun went down, the moon bathed the battlefield in pale light making the task of recovering the wounded hazardous. In consequence wounded men, that might have been saved by prompt medical attention, died of their wounds in the night.

One of the men who did manage to make it back to his own lines was Sergeant Robert Philip from Leith who had been hit in the leg during the charge and could not go on. A short distance in front of him he had seen Lieutenant Frank Thompson, another of the Gretna survivors, badly hit but continuing to give orders to his men. Robert Philip found that he was lying in an exposed position and so intense was the rifle fire around him that he was hit a further three times while he lay on the ground, luckily not seriously. However, he had lost both his water bottle and his emergency rations and now was faint with loss of blood. With the battle continuing to rage around him he knew that no stretcher bearer would come, so he had been forced to lie there in the fierce heat all that day and all through the night, too weak and disoriented to move.

But by the time dawn broke he had recovered a little strength and so drawing on his last reserves of energy he resolved to crawl to where he could see smoke rising from an encampment some little distance away. He could not tell whether it were a British or a Turkish position, but if the latter, he told himself, he still had his rifle and ten rounds of ammunition and resolved to take his chance. He was lucky: it was men from the reinforcing Hampshires who had moved up during the night.

The Hampshires also rescued Private Daniel Page who said he regretted that he had not been able to fire a single bullet in the charge for as he reached the first Turkish trench his right hand had been shot away, the bullet also wrecking the magazine of his rifle. As he had struggled up from where he had fallen, he had been shot again, this time in the arm and immediately after that felt some 'awful blow' on his knee. Looking down at his leg he saw that the knee cap and most of the bone behind had been carried away by what he thought must have been shrapnel.

Too injured now to move, he managed to roll himself into some shrubbery where he lay all that day and all the night and all the next day, more than thirty hours in all, half mad with thirst and too weak to move until eventually he was found.

FIFTY

As the Royal Scots rested after the battle, they received a message from Major-General de Lisle, who commanded the 87th Brigade which had broken through as planned a mile over the coastal plateau. 'Well done Royal Scots,' it read. General Sir Ian Hamilton, Commander in Chief of the British forces, also recognised the Royal Scots battle prowess, making a personal visit to thank the battalion for its splendid work. Regular soldiers in the 87th brigade had their own words of praise. 'These Scotch Terriers are fair devils,' they said.

But whether the result was worth the appalling cost was doubtful. As a consequence of the attacks on 28 June, the British front had pivoted near the centre so that it had been advanced a mile further along the coast and a triangular wedge of territory had been gained. Four lines of Turkish trenches had been captured with 200 prisoners, 3 mountain guns and an immense quantity of ammunition.

Turkish losses in men were heavy matching, if not exceeding, the British. Intelligence reports put the numbers of Turkish dead at over 5,000 with three times as many more wounded. In total some 86,000 Turkish soldiers died defending their homeland against the invaders at Gallipoli.

If the Royal Scots asked themselves whether this was really the bold strategic move to circumvent stalemate on the Western front that had been intended, they could rest content they had done all that they had been asked and more besides. Leith could be proud of them.

And Leith was proud of them, but uncomprehending, too. As the news of the great attack of 28th of June 1915 filtered back home, elation among the public at the success of their soldier sons was soon replaced by sorrow as the extent of the casualties became known. The lists of those killed grew daily as more and more of the injured died of their wounds.

On August 4th the *Leith Burghs Pilot* published a list of 200 casualties from the 7th Royal Scots' action but it did not say whether these men had been killed, wounded or were missing in action. In each succeeding issue the paper published supplementary lists as the full extent of the battle became known. Many of those initially listed as missing or wounded now figured in the lists of the dead. Leith was plunged into mourning for the second time in barely more than a month.

Such was the slaughter among the officers that people could only think that some great unforeseen tragedy had occurred - a second Gretna. At that stage of the war people were not accustomed to the terrible casualty lists that would accompany many later battles. Certainly they would not have realised that without artillery support the

Royal Scots had accomplished the rare feat of carrying all their objectives against a resolute and gallant enemy, well dug in and fighting in defence of his homeland. But this was scarce compensation for the devastating loss of life.

Within two weeks of landing the two companies of the 7th Royal Scots plus the five officers from A and D companies who had survived the Gretna disaster had been reduced to 170 men (out of some 450) and 5 officers out of 20 who had disembarked.

The 4th Battalion suffered on a similar scale, and as both battalions were now so severely reduced and had lost so many senior officers, what was left of them combined as a single composite unit under Colonel Peebles' command. After spending a few days recuperating in the reserve trenches, they were again sent out to the front line but this time they saw no serious fighting.

Even now there was to be no respite, for a week later they were sent forward again to take part in another punishing attack. Leaving camp at 3am, the composite battalion marched out up the peninsular to take positions in the reserve trenches 400 yards behind the front line where two brigades lay waiting to attack Turkish trenches at the foot of Achi Baba.

The attack started after a heavy artillery bombardment at 7.35am and would probably have met with complete success if the leading troops, after taking two trenches, had not gone forward again, in accordance with their orders to assault a third which in the event proved not to exist. This intelligence failure resulted in many casualties for the troops were then caught in the open and mown down by machine gun fire as they made their way back.

In the desire to get forward the first two trenches had not been properly cleared. Ordered forward at this point it became the job of the 4th and 7th Royal Scots to clear these two trenches who once more found themselves in a fierce battle which continued until the Turks were finally flushed out.

Again the casualties were heavy. The 4th Royal Scots were fortunate in not losing any further officers but they took another 74 casualties in other ranks, while the 7th Royal Scotts lost Second Lieutenant Lyell. The Gretna survivor, Lieutenant Haws, was also killed that day. Among the 170 other ranks, that remained standing after the attack on the 28th June, the 7th lost a further 51 men.

What was left of the composite battalion now laboured on in the captured trenches, repulsing Turkish counter-attacks until July 15th when eventually they were relieved. After a day spent clearing away and burying the dead, Peebles led his enfeebled force back to the rest camp where they stayed for the remainder of the month.

In early August, in an attempt to bypass the stalemate that had been reached in the south, a new phase of the Gallipoli campaign opened with landings at Suvla Bay in the middle of the European side of the peninsular. This achieved some success at first, but then the attack started to run out of steam and a new stalemate resulted. Large numbers of troops were brought up from the south to participate in these attacks and as a result the Royal Scots had to undergo long periods of unrelieved duty in the southern trenches.

About this time some of the officers who had been injured at Gretna arrived in Gallipoli to rejoin the battalion and as this coincided with the arrival of a further 12 officers and 440 other ranks from the second line of the 7th Royal Scots, the battalion resumed its former separate identity and morale increased markedly.

But with the failure of the Suvla Bay campaign, a mood of pessimism began to descend which affected both commanders and their men. As Major Ewing was to report in his 'History of the Royal Scots,' *'From that time onwards a want of confidence clouded the minds of the leaders of the enterprise and it was not immediately clear what the next step should be. Unfortunately, there was good reason for pessimism. The principal design of the campaign had been to circumvent the deadlock that had arisen on the Western Front and the most convincing evidence of its breakdown was the undoubted fact that a deadlock had also been reached in Gallipoli; opposing lines of trench systems, as in France, covered the ground at Cape Helles and at Suvla Bay. It seemed as though all possibility of effecting a surprise had been dissipated, and if we were to secure our objects by a series of trench to trench attacks we should require a far larger number of men and a much greater supply of heavy guns and shells than we had at the peninsular. But if this was the prerequisite of success, it was at least questionable if it were worthwhile persevering with the campaign. For the cost in life would necessarily be heavy, and it might serve our purpose better to concentrate on one front instead of two, and if this were so, Gallipoli would have to be abandoned.'*

Thus reasoned the leaders of the campaign which had cost British, Anzac and French casualties running into the hundreds of thousands. After August and the failure of the Suvla Bay attack there were therefore no more major initiatives in Gallipoli and preparations for withdrawal began.

FIFTY-ONE

Back in Scotland, the final act of the Gretna tragedy was now about to be played out. On Tuesday 15 September 1915, the three railwaymen indicted by Coroner Strong's court stood trial at the High Court of Judiciary in Edinburgh. The hearing lasted a day and a half and for both days the court was packed with many members of the public being turned away.

The trial was a weighty affair, presided over by Lord Strathclyde, the Lord Justice-General of Scotland. The Crown brought in the Lord Advocate, Robert Munro QC, MP, to lead for the prosecution, thereby demonstrating the importance the authorities attached to this case. Mr Condie Sandeman led for the defence and among those in court was Mr JE Williams, General-Secretary of the National Union of Railwaymen. The charge was culpable homicide against Meakin, Tinsley and Hutchinson.

Meakin was charged specifically with 'failure to use a lever collar in the specified manner to prevent the up line signal being drawn, and with failing to give the '*blocking back'* signal.' Tinsley was charged with 'accepting the troop train without first ascertaining that the line was clear,' and with 'late arrival at the signal box on the morning in question.' Hutchinson was charged with 'leaving the signal box without first receiving an assurance that the line was protected by a lever collar on the signal.'

The Clerk of the Court proceeded: *'The accused are further charged by respective breaches of duty, or one or more of them, with having caused the special troop train to collide with the local passenger train, and to be run into by an express train from Carlisle to Glasgow, and did thus kill Herbert Henry Ford, engineer, 49 Stewarton Drive, Cambuslang; Samuel Stephen Dyer, railway saloon car attendant, Lorne Road, Wealdstone, London; James Crawford Bonnar, Lieutenant, Argyll and Sutherland Highlanders, 16 Queen Street, Helensburgh; Francis William Scott, passenger train driver, 2 Etterby Road, Carlisle; James Hannah, train fireman, 11 Scaurbank Road, Carlisle; and others.'*

All three men pleaded 'Not Guilty.' The defence led no evidence at the trial and the two signalmen were therefore spared the pain of cross-examination. The circumstances which had led up to the accident were described by the other witnesses called by the prosecution and from these Mr Condie Sandeman tried to extract, in cross-examination, some mitigating circumstances. Thus Robert Killin, the Caledonian's Assistant Superintendent, agreed that the signalmen had been a good many years in the Company's service, were men of good character and were excellent employees. Alexander Thorburn, the Gretna stationmaster said that he had found Tinsley and Meakin to be satisfactory men, experienced and competent. And although Sandeman tried to press Robert Killin to admit that the extra wartime traffic might have been a factor, Killin would only say that a signalman on a Saturday morning in May in present conditions would be no busier than on a peacetime Saturday in August. He thought the men should have been quite able to do the work.

Nor did Mr Sandeman get much joy out of the District Traffic Inspector, William McAlpine, when he questioned him about the frequency with which lever collars were used. If Condie Sandeman had hoped that the Inspector would have agreed there had been other times when these collars had not been employed then it was not to be. He had never been into a box and seen that the collar was not on when it should have been, he declared, and this case was, in his experience, *'quite unique.'*

When the trial opened for the second day there remained to give evidence only Thomas Ingram and the two engine drivers of the express who just just repeated what they had said before. So, after evidence relating to the identification of the dead had been given, the prosecution rested its case.

Condie Sandeman now moved that the judge might direct the jury that there was no evidence against Hutchinson, as indeed none had been given by the prosecution's witnesses and the Lord Advocate, whether deliberately or nor, had not sought to draw any. He told the Judge that he thought Hutchinson was entitled to a verdict of 'not guilty,' and the Lord Advocate concurred. Lord Strathclyde indicated his assent and said he would direct the Jury to find Hutchinson 'not guilty.' He would, however, for now remain in the dock.

The Lord Advocate then addressed the Jury on behalf of the prosecution and asked for a guilty verdict against Meakin and Tinsley.

'The case, he said, *'was worthy of the greatest possible care......because of the appalling loss of life which resulted from the collision. We only have to reflect for a moment on the fields of Gretna, on that bright summer morning like the fields of Flanders. You have only for a moment to reflect on the high hopes in those brave hearts which were quenched suddenly that morning, of the desolation which was brought into countless homes, in order to appreciate at once the awfulness of the catastrophe, the cause of which it is your duty to ascertain. The case.....was also important from the point of view of the travelling public.......the two men in the dock were not ignorant men or drawn from the criminal classes. They were men of ripe experience and .....of admitted competence. ...Tremendous responsibilities.....rested upon railway signalmen.......They were there to administer a code of rules which had been drawn up.....for the sole purpose of protecting the travelling public from injury......It was the Jury's duty to say whether, on this*

occasion....the rules of the railway company were not flagrantly violated.

'The material facts of the case were largely not in dispute. The first charge against Meakin was that he failed to make use of a lever collar, and the second charge was that he failed to use the 'blocking back' signal. They were charges of serious, grave, vital omissions.......When the local train was moved from the main line to the other it became imperative that the signalman should put the lever collar on the lever which worked the home signal.......breach of duty in this respect was abundantly clear.

'Was there any doubt that the man who failed to perform that duty was Meakin? It might be suggested that it was not clear it was Meakin whose duty it was to give the 'blocking back' signal and put on the lever collar. But that would not do. In the first place it was clear that it was the duty of the man who put the local train on the main line to protect that train from injury by the means provided. It was proved beyond all doubt that the duty was not performed and that the man who failed to perform it was Meakin.

'The charges against Tinsley were that he accepted the troop train in the circumstances then existing, and he lowered the signal to enable the troop train to pass. He had forgotten about the existence of the train on which a few minutes before he had himself travelled from Carlisle. He forgot about a train which was then a few feet from him if he had looked out of the window.....That it was a *grave breach of duty to do so was also a matter which was not capable of argument. The local train was there, under his eyes, on the line on which he had given the 'line-clear' signal to Kirkpatrick to send through the troop train. That was a gross breach of duty and that Tinsley was responsible for it he did not himself dispute.*

'The duty of signalmen was not to rely upon the block telegraph system alone, but to use their own eyesight to see that the signals were clear....There might be a suggestion that if Meakin had done his duty, Tinsley would have been all right. That kind of argument would not do. Tinsley had acted not only contrary to the rule but to the ordinary dictates of prudence. The Jury....would find the origin of the whole disaster in the clandestine arrangement between the two signalmen.

'I think you would agree that it would be quite intolerable if these valuable human lives, dear to their friends and invaluable to their country at the moment when it happened, should be imperilled and sacrificed. Why? In order that a signalman may spend half an hour more between the sheets on a particular morning. It seems to me that this is not overstating the case with regard to Tinsley. My suggestion is that if the arrangement had not subsisted, none of us would be here today and much valuable life would have been preserved. A verdict in favour of the accused in this case would be rightly interpreted as a charter of indemnity to railway officials to disregard the rules provided by the Company, if they so pleased.'

FIFTY-TWO

Opening for the defence, Mr Condie Sandeman attacked the Lord Advocate's colourful remarks. He had not got his gift of eloquence, he told the Jury, nor would he talk of summer mornings, fields of Flanders, desolated homes and things like that. But he was glad that he did not have that eloquence, because it seemed that when one had it, one would exercise it, and one exercised a gift like that for no other purpose than to produce prejudice, and to induce people to decide matter, not on the facts, but emotional feelings that should be absent from a court of justice.

Tinsley and Meakin, the day before the accident, were described as workmen of the highest class who, for periods of ten and eight years respectively, had done their duty faithfully. The Lord Advocate was now asking the Jury to find that the men were criminals and to have them sent to prison where they would be of no use to anyone, and their careers ruined.

He went on to say that criminals were judged by their intention to commit crime; except in the case of criminal negligence or culpable homicide, where a man might do something half a dozen times and be merely judged a careless fellow; but if death resulted, then he would become guilty of a crime. Therefore a little negligence would not do, it must be some very gross negligence which directly contributed to the result.

'The charges are two in number against Meakin. The first was that he did not put a lever collar on the lever controlling the signal, and the second is that he did not give the 'blocking back' signal. In the matter of the collar, the Lord Advocate had said that Meakin admitted to Mr Killin that he did not put it on, and added 'as he ought to have done.' Meakin made no admission whatever that it was his duty to put the lever collar on in the circumstances. There happened to be a difference of opinion among the witnesses as to whether the collar should have been put on.....'

(It is far from clear what evidence Mr Sandeman was referring to here as no such inconsistency appears in the transcripts of evidence). However he went on to make a few salient points in Meakin's defence.

'When the local was shunted on to the up main line it was already protected by the fact that the signal 'out of section' in reference to the Welsh train had not been given and the line was not signalled as clear. It was not proved that the collar ought to have been put on by Meakin when the train was put there. The critical thing came to be, who was it who gave the 'out of section' signal to Kirkpatrick? Was it Meakin or was it not? They must answer that before they could say he was guilty. It might have been Tinsley. They had got to be satisfied that the signal had

304

been passed back by Meakin: how could they satisfy themselves about that?

'Meakin, of course, admitted putting through the local train and putting the Welsh goods train into the loop. If Meakin did not give the 'out of section' signal, it was not necessary for him to give the 'blocking back' signal. In a state of evidence like that they could not find a man guilty of gross negligence which involved the consequences of crime.'

It was a pity that the two signalmen were not defended by separate lawyers for the signalmen's interests were by no means identical. Meakin might have been defended (and perhaps should have been defended rather better than he was) by pointing out that the sequence of safety operations - 'train out of section,' 'blocking back,' lever collar - were physically interrupted by Tinsley going straight to the block and therefore assuming responsibility for them. Meakin would no doubt have strongly resented Tinsley standing over him instructing him to send 'blocking back' signals and to use lever collars and the reverse situation would also surely have applied that morning. You don't tell your mate his job. Besides Meakin had at that point already been on continuous duty for 10 and a half hours (caused by Tinsley's lateness) and no doubt was eager for his break. Such a defence for Meakin, however, would necessarily throw the whole culpability on to Tinsley. Equally, defending Tinsley involved holding Meakin responsible for the various lapses in safety procedures. Nevertheless Mr Sandeman had to defend both men as best he could.

'Tinsley,' he argued, 'was the man who actually accepted the troop train....He signalled 'line clear' when the line was obstructed......Was that negligence, or was it something else......that was not negligence? That was one of those sudden curious lapses of memory that were so completely recognised by the railway company that they had added two or three precautions to try to cure what they saw was inevitable when the human element was introduced....It would not be negligence if he fell down in an epileptic fit. He had the misfortune suddenly to forget about the train, and he had the further misfortune that there was no collar upon the lever; and further that the indicator of the telegraph showed 'line clear.' These two things further misled him. In other words the very perfection of the system was against him because, the more perfect the system, the less men relied upon themselves and the more they relied upon the system - that was, in the end, on other men.*

Sandeman concluded by telling the Jury, 'Of course there was fault; but it could not be said that these men were responsible, and the only course before them was to return a verdict of not guilty.'

And with that strange conclusion that the signalmen were not responsible for their actions, he sat down. He had managed to defend them both only by incriminating them both, so they would now stand or fall together.

FIFTY-THREE

The Lord Justice-General now began to sum up. There had rarely been a clearer or more simple case, he said. The material facts were undisputed and clear. There were many degrees of culpable homicide, but that was for him to consider. If the Jury were satisfied that by the gross negligence of these men, these valuable lives had been lost, then they must find them guilty.

It was indisputable that somebody was to blame, he continued. That somebody's fault had brought about this deplorable catastrophe. There were no unfavourable conditions of weather, and no neglect on the part of the railway company to provide what was necessary for the safety of the travelling public. He turned to Meakin..

'Meakin said that he did not give the 'blocking back' signal; he admitted not having put on the lever collar. It was the man who directed the local train to leave the down main and go to the up main whose duty it was to put on the lever collar and to give the 'blocking back' signal. They could easily see for themselves that it would never do to

leave such an imperative and insistent duty to any subsequent incomer into the signal box.'

Accordingly he must direct the Jury, he said, that if the evidence showed that the lever collar had not been put on and the blocking back signal had not been given, it was Meakin who had failed in his duty. As for Tinsley...

'Tinsley travelled on the local train. He left the local train as it was in the process of shunting and went to the signal box to take up duty. A few minutes afterwards he was asked to accept a troop train coming from the north. He accepted it and signalled that the line was perfectly clear. It was for the jury to say if that was not to neglect his duty. No doubt he said he forgot. It was for the jury to say whether they could accept such an excuse as that from a highly intelligent man, a man who knew his duty thoroughly and who had been many years on that duty.'

He then turned to Tinsley's late arrival in the box.

'It appears that Meakin and Tinsley made an arrangement.....that Tinsley should come on duty somewhat later than his appointed time....in breach of regulations.....If Tinsley had not been able to travel with the local train he would have been very nearly an hour late that morning.'

He did not, however, proceed to conclude anything from this, but told the Jury that, in all probability the accident would not have happened but for the clandestine arrangement to change shift at a different hour to the one laid down. As for the signalmen previously being of good conduct, he said that it was not the jury's duty to inquire into their past characters. Railway companies were not, after all, in the habit of placing men in signalboxes who were not up to the job. The jury's duty was rather to.. *'say whether on that day and at that time they were guilty and brought about these deplorable results.'* With that he concluded; the jury retired to consider their verdict. The time was twenty minutes to one.

They were back a mere eight minutes later. Hutchinson was found not guilty as directed; Tinsley and Meakin were found guilty on all points.

Hutchinson was at last dismissed from the dock and the Lord Advocate moved for sentence on Meakin and Tinsley. At this Mr Smith Clark, Junior Counsel for the defence, rose and asked the Judge to consider the prisoners' position. Each of them had, he said, suffered in a shocking fashion. They had had a nervous breakdown and had suffered from sleeplessness and mental anguish. Taking everything into consideration he asked his Lordship to impose as lenient a sentence as he might think proper.

The point was not lost. In passing sentence Lord Strathclyde said that, for his part, he would do nothing to add to the bitterness and lifelong remorse the prisoners must feel at the thought of the awful consequences of their gross breach of duty of which they had been convicted. He saw room for drawing a distinction in the cases and therefore passed a sentence of eighteen months imprisonment on Meakin, and three years penal servitude on Tinsley. Heads bowed the two ex-signalmen were led away from the dock.

A year later, with full remission, Meakin completed his sentence and was released from prison and although Tinsley still had another year to serve, the authorities were compassionate and released him, too. The two men made their way back to the Border.

Tinsley's fear of losing his railway cottage proved unfounded for the Caledonian let him keep it; more than that, the Company later offered to re-employ both men, although not as signalmen, and both accepted. Tinsley became a lampman and porter at Carlisle in which capacity he worked humbly for another 30 years until he reached retiring age. He died in 1967.

Meakin became a 'second man,' working in the guard's van on pick-up goods trains and later set him himself up in business as a coal merchant. Though this business seems initially to have been successful it eventually collapsed, no doubt due to the economic depression. Meakin ended his career doing clerical work at the Gretna munitions factory, reopened as an ammunition depot in the 1930s, where he rose to become head of the office. He died n 1953.

FIFTY-FOUR

In Gallipoli the hot days of summer gave way to the cooler nights of autumn and then to torrential winter rains. The Royal Scots continued to lose men in minor skirmishes and as a result of the depredations of enemy snipers, a tragic waste exacerbated by the scourge of dysentery.

October brought a foretaste of winter conditions with rain that fell so heavily that it seemed to form wires of steel in the air and turned the dust into thick, clinging mud, which filled the dugouts of the trenches and the shelters of the rest camp. Although the men had been issued with waterproof sheets these were of no use against such heavy rain. Flooded out of their shelters and unable to sleep, the Royal Scots tramped about at nights to relieve the cold and quicken the circulation.

November brought snow. One terrible storm lasted for three days and ravaged the peninsular with a fury that threatened to destroy every living soul as Allied and Turkish troops alike cowed in the mud-filled trenches, more frightened of the weather than of each other. Rain, sleet and snow, whipped by a hurricane, beat madly on Gallipoli as if Heaven wanted to avenge and efface the

311

appalling loss of human life there. Soldiers reported the sensation of their bodies being laced by a thousand needles of ice, while tumultuous seas beat along the coast, booming and crashing as they smashed the recently constructed piers and the lighters moored below them and littered the beaches with their wreckage.

It was not until January that the weather improved sufficiently for the final evacuation to take place and, in the event, it proved to be by far the most successful of all of the Gallipoli operations, being accomplished without the loss of a single life. Though no soldier was sorry to see the last of those low hills and ridges, all left with a feeling of profound loss for the many good friends and comrades that they had left behind, their blood so needlessly spilt in an ill-omened and unnecessary exercise that had ended in stalemate and defeat.

All the stores that could not be transported were now set alight and from the decks of the battleship *Prince George,* the Royal Scots watched the flames leap skyward in the darkness. And behind the flames summit of Achi Baba stood out against the night sky like a guardian over the peninsular.

After Gallipoli the battalion once more travelled eastwards to fight this time in Palestine, where two of the Gretna survivors, Captain Weir and Captain Wightman, the latter now recovered from his Gallipoli wound, fell during the second battle for Gaza in 1917.

Only three officers came through Gretna and Gallipoli without injury. Lieutenant-Colonel Peebles continued to command the battalion until 1917 when he returned to take up a home posting after two years of continuous front-line service. Having also escaped injury Captain A.M. Mitchell received his Majority and then was promoted again to Lieutenant-Colonel in which rank he assumed command of the 4th Royal Scots. Captain Romanes was also promoted Major and later took command of the 7th Scottish Rifles in Egypt.

Back in Leith Provost Malcolm Smith's Memorial Committee eventually attracted £4,000 in subscriptions - upwards of a quarter of a million in today's money - and Mr George Simpson, the Leith Burgh architect, was invited to design a memorial. It stands today - a fine tall Celtic Cross, carved from red granite after the fashion of the Cross of St Martin on Iona.

On its stem the lion rampant of Scotland stood proud when it was installed at Rosebank Cemetery and, on the wall behind, in two ornate stone frames, were set ten great plaques of bronze recoding the 214 names of those Royal Scots who died in the Gretna tragedy.

The Edinburgh and Leith Cemetery Company, the owners of Rosebank had felt it their duty to 'assist in the commemoration of the sad event.' In a letter to Provost Smith they therefore wrote that *'the ground now forms a place of sad interest to very many people and already visitors had come long distances to view the spot where the victims of the disaster are interred.'*

In the circumstances the Directors felt they should show their sympathy in practical form and they therefore now offered the military authorities, free of any charge, the ground to accommodate the memorial.

The dedication ceremony took place on Sunday 16 May 1916, almost exactly a year after the accident and once more Provost Smith and the Magistrates and Councillors of Leith paraded with the Scottish military command and with the relatives of many of the soldiers who had died that day. After a brief service, Lord Roseberry, the regiment's Colonel in Chief unveiled the ten great bronze plaques as the people watched and remembered the sadness of the past year.

At the base of the Cross they read an inscription in bronze which Lord Roseberry had composed himself. In doing so he may have had in mind the fate, not only of those in 'A' and 'D' companies who had died in the troop train, but those in 'B' and 'C' companies who had suffered a similar fate in the Gallipoli dust only a month later. It read:

IN MEMORY OF OFFICERS, NON-COMMISSIONED OFFICERS AND MEN, 7TH BATTALION THE ROYAL SCOTS, LEITH TERRITORIAL BATTALION, WHO MET THEIR DEATH AT GRETNA ON MAY 22ND 1915 IN A TERRIBLE RAILWAY DISASTER ON THEIR WAY TO FIGHT FOR THEIR COUNTRY.

THIS MEMORIAL AND A BED IN LEITH HOSPITAL, ARE DEDICATED BY MOURNING COMRADES AND FRIENDS.

YEA, THOUGH I WALK THROUGH THE VALLEY OF THE SHADOW OF DEATH, I WILL FEAR NO EVIL FOR THOU ART WITH ME.

Lightning Source UK Ltd.
Milton Keynes UK
UKOW04f1234260814

237590UK00011B/292/P